MODERN WORLD NATIONS

Honduras

Updated Edition

Roger E. Dendinger

Series Editor
Charles F. Gritzner
South Dakota State University

CHELSEA HOUSE
An Infobase Learning Company

Frontispiece: Flag of Honduras

Cover: Iglesia Los Dolores (Church of the Sorrows), Tegicigalpa, Honduras

Honduras, Updated Edition

Copyright © 2012 by Infobase Publishing

Chelsea House
An imprint of Infobase Learning
132 West 31st Street
New York NY 10001

The Library of Congress has catalogued the earlier edition as follows:
Dendinger, Roger.
  Honduras / Roger E. Dendinger.
    p. cm.—(Modern world nations)
  Includes bibliographical references and index.
  ISBN-13: 978–0-7910–9510–2 (hardcover)
  ISBN-10: 0–7910–9510–X (hardcover)
  1. Honduras—Juvenile literature. I. Title. II. Series.

  F1758.5.D46 2007
  972.83—dc22   2007026440
  ISBN 978-1-61753-046-3

Chelsea House books are available at special discounts when purchased in bulk quantities for businesses, associations, institutions, or sales promotions. Please call our Special Sales Department in New York at (212) 967-8800 or (800) 322-8755.

You can find Chelsea House on the World Wide Web at
http://www.infobaselearning.com

Series design by Takeshi Takahashi
Cover design by Jooyoung An
Cover printed by Bang Printing, Brainerd, Minn.
Book printed and bound by Bang Printing, Brainerd, Minn.
Date printed: November 2011

Printed in the United States of America

This book is printed on acid-free paper.

All links and Web addresses were checked and verified to be correct at the time of publication. Because of the dynamic nature of the Web, some addresses and links may have changed since publication and may no longer be valid.

Table of Contents

Honduras

Updated Edition

Introducing Honduras

"Honduras" evokes images of tropical rain forests, misty mountains, Caribbean beaches, and hospitable people living in poverty. Apart from these stereotypes, what else comes to mind when you hear the word *Honduras*? The country is one of several in this part of the world that share fundamental physical and cultural characteristics. In the past, these similarities often blurred the distinctions among the region's countries. Many outsiders fail to distinguish Honduras as a specific place in tropical Central America.

In some ways, this identity problem is reflected in the history of Honduras. During its colonial period and then through the early era of independence, Honduras struggled to create its own place within the Spanish colonial and postcolonial world. Today, Honduras still struggles to assert its cultural independence from its neighbors but at the same time cooperates with them economically for mutual benefit.

Common physical characteristics underpin the more significant cultural similarities that Honduras shares with nearby countries. Part of the great land bridge linking North and South America, Honduras shares borders with Guatemala, El Salvador, and Nicaragua. Striking physical features and sharp environmental contrasts are found throughout this part of the world. Like Guatemala and Nicaragua, Honduras's Caribbean coast is hot and wet year-round. Its short Pacific coast is seasonally dry. Remnants of rain forest create a discontinuous band linking Honduras with Guatemala to the west and Nicaragua to the east. Relatively cool highlands in the interior have always attracted most Honduran settlement.

Honduras shares many natural hazards with its neighbors. The famous "Ring of Fire," a series of geologically young volcanic mountain ranges girdling the Pacific Ocean, runs through Central America. Most of the large active volcanoes in the region are found in Guatemala and Nicaragua, but Honduras shares the dramatic volcanic landscapes for which Central America is famous. The Ring of Fire also is associated with earthquake activity. Recently, most of the worst quakes in the region have been in Nicaragua and El Salvador. Honduras is routinely affected by small quakes, though, and occasionally larger and more devastating ones.

The greatest natural hazard occurs seasonally from June to November. Honduras lies in the southernmost portion of the Western Hemisphere's hurricane zone. Because of its location relative to areas of hurricane formation and typical storm tracks, it tends to receive some of the worst storms that strike Central America. One of the most destructive in history struck Honduras in 1998. Hurricane Mitch will always be remembered for the suffering it brought to Honduras, as well as to Nicaragua and Guatemala.

In terms of cultural similarities, Honduras shares with its Central American neighbors a language, a religion, a popular culture, and a long colonial history. The Spanish colonizers

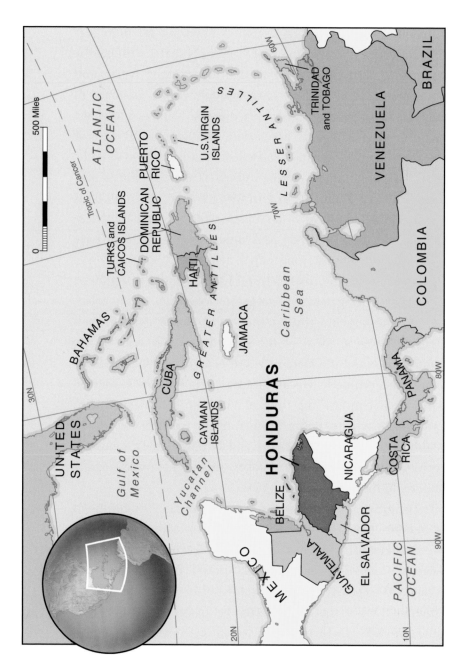

Honduras is located in Central America and shares borders with the countries of Guatemala to the west, El Salvador to the southwest, and Nicaragua to the southeast. In addition, the Caribbean Sea borders it to the north, and the Gulf of Fonseca serves as its southern border, between El Salvador and Nicaragua.

who came in the sixteenth century planted a monolithic system of administration that stretched from Mexico through the Andes Mountains of South America. The Spanish language was the universal tongue of government, education, business, and the Roman Catholic Church throughout this vast area. During the colonial era, Honduras competed several times with Guatemala and El Salvador to be the site of the *audiencia*, the seat of colonial government in the northern portion of this New World Empire. The far richer colonies always won. After independence came in the early nineteenth century, Honduras was at the center of attempts to form regional unions. Again, though, its neighbors who were more powerful politically dominated the planning and organization of these unions. In the end, however, all of the attempts failed.

A blurring of national identity has characterized Honduras from the beginnings of its independence. In part, this problem is left over from the Spanish era. Borders were carelessly defined by colonial administrators. They lacked the political significance we think of as being essential to a country's survival today. After independence, however, boundaries came to define the fate of the new Central American republics as each of the former colonies was thrown back on its own physical resources. Political geographers often assert that a sure test of sovereignty is a state's ability to control its borders and territory. Honduras and its neighbors have often failed this test.

Along with a blurred national identity and vaguely defined national boundaries, abandonment is a theme in the country's history. For centuries, outsiders came into Honduras, taking what they wanted, and then leaving. First the Spanish found gold and silver in Central America and moved from place to place, developing, then abandoning mining facilities as the minerals ran out. Colonial rulers brought people in to work the mines and then left them stranded once the mining activity moved to another colony. In the nineteenth century, low-lying coastal areas came under the control of foreign banana companies. They also moved from place to place, creating jobs, then moved on to other countries without regard to the problems they were leaving behind.

In the twentieth century, blurred national identity and vague borders continued to plague the region. Honduras became involved in the internal political intrigues of Guatemala, El Salvador, and Nicaragua, with disastrous consequences. Coups, insurrections, and wars occurred, and refugees routinely spilled across the contested borders of the region. These patterns of political interference and interaction among the Central American republics came about in large part because of the common culture and ethnicity of the people living in them. As in other parts of Central America, Honduras has a large population of people of mixed blood. Descendents of Spanish colonizers and Amerindians, these *mestizos* have suffered centuries of discrimination and sometimes repression throughout Latin America. At times in the recent past, military dictatorships made them second-class citizens in their own countries. In Honduras, the inequalities that grew up around social divisions are still serious problems.

Many of the qualities that hinder twenty-first-century growth are the same features that disadvantaged the country in the past. After gold mining declined in the late sixteenth century, Honduras suffered from colonial neglect. Other parts of the Spanish New World held the riches and resources colonial administrators were searching for. Honduras's Caribbean coast lacked good natural harbors, and most of the good farmland lay far inland. Labor shortages were common, as the only means of employment were a few struggling cattle ranches and small mines. As part of the Viceroyalty of New Spain, a large territory centered on Mexico City, Honduras came to be perceived as an unimportant place unlucky in its location and its settlement.

Despite its unfortunate past, Honduras today is not content to muddle along as it has. A new generation of leaders is planning a future that will bring the country into a closer and more equitable relationship with its near neighbors as well as with

Approximately 7 percent of Hondurans are considered Amerindian, including the Garifuna, who are the descendants of escaped slaves and Carib Indians. Here, a young Garifuna boy eats a coconut near his home in the Honduran coastal village of Miami.

the United States. After almost two centuries of failed attempts at creating a regional union, the dream of a United States of Central America is still alive. The form that it takes today, however, is very different from the idealistic notions that motivated leaders in the nineteenth century. Today, union among the republics of the region is perceived in strictly economic terms. Free trade, or at least freer trade, among the Central American states and between them and the United States is the goal of Honduran leaders. Currently, a long-range vision of the country as a place of regional economic integration motivates Honduras's leaders to promote foreign investment and industrial development. The short-term adjustments necessary to open the economy to global trade may be painful for some, but future gains will benefit the country as a whole.

Plans for a more prosperous future are under way, and modest progress has been accomplished. The past has left its mark on the country, however. Honduras was one of the original "banana republics," a derisive term for Central American countries dependent on agricultural exports to the United States. Much of its early twentieth-century infrastructure—railroad, telegraph lines, and ports—was built and controlled by U.S. interests, principally the United Fruit Company. Like its Mayan heritage, this aspect of the country's past is still alive. Despite economic advances during the past decade, Honduras is still dependent on banana, coffee, and sugarcane production for much of its export revenue.

What, then, can an outsider make of such a complicated place? To begin with, an understanding of the country's physical setting is important. In the second chapter, we will identify the possibilities and the limitations posed by the natural environment. Keeping in mind that the past is prologue to the future, Chapter 3 outlines the historical geography of the pre-European people, the Spanish colonizers, and the rise of an independent Honduras. A profile of the people and culture of Honduras is the subject of Chapter 4. The next two chapters describe the government and economy of the country. Chapter 7 takes you on a tour of regional contrasts, and the final chapter examines the economics of development and the potential changes that Honduras faces once it joins the world community of trade and competition.

2

Physical Landscapes

Imagine a wedge of territory shaped like a rough convex polygon, or, more imaginatively, like an irregularly drawn *sensu*, or folding Japanese hand fan. The longest side of the polygon is Honduras's northern coast. It stretches along the Caribbean Sea for 400 miles (645 kilometers), from the Gulf of Honduras in the west to the Mosquito Coast in the east. The shortest side is the southern coastline. Only 40 miles (65 kilometers) long, it borders the Gulf of Fonseca, an inlet of the Pacific Ocean. The second-largest Central American country, Honduras occupies 43,277 square miles (112,087 square kilometers), making it slightly smaller than the U.S. state of Ohio. Within this wedge of land, a traveler may find long uninhabited beaches, rugged mountains, mangrove swamps, and rain forests. Earthquakes routinely rock the steep slopes in the interior, and hurricanes reshape the coastal plain every few years.

Almost half of Honduras's international borders are formed by rivers. The Río Goascorán and the Río Lempa define a portion of the border between El Salvador and Honduras. To the east, the Río Coco marks nearly half of the long, isolated border between Nicaragua and Honduras.

The shape and size of the national territory, its varied natural landscapes, and its tropical location explain the unexpected beauty of Honduras, as well as many of the challenges it faces as a growing country.

Honduras lies entirely within the tropics, that region of Earth extending from the equator north to the Tropic of Cancer (23 1/2° north latitude) and south to the Tropic of Capricorn (23 1/2° south latitude). This planet-encircling belt of low-latitude land and sea is sometimes known as the Torrid Zone. Here, the sun is high in the sky year-round. The amount of radiant energy the Earth receives from the sun is generally greatest at the equator and in the tropics. This results in very warm temperatures year-round. Still, tropical regions do contain dramatic differences in temperature and rainfall. The image we sometimes have of the tropics as perpetually hot and wet is not always accurate. Some parts of the Torrid Zone experience dry seasons and lack the lush vegetation we think of as typical of "tropical jungles." Other parts lie high above sea level, far from the moderating effects of the world's oceans. Because topography plays a central role in explaining tropical climate patterns, we will look at elevation to get a sense of the variety of local physical conditions in Honduras.

ALTITUDINAL LIFE ZONES

In the tropics, as in other regions, differences in elevation determine such physical characteristics of the land as rainfall, soils, vegetation, and animal life. Geographers correlate elevation and temperature to create a generalized scheme for describing tropical microclimates. Altitudinal zonation, or altitudinal life zones, is the name for this scheme that helps us understand

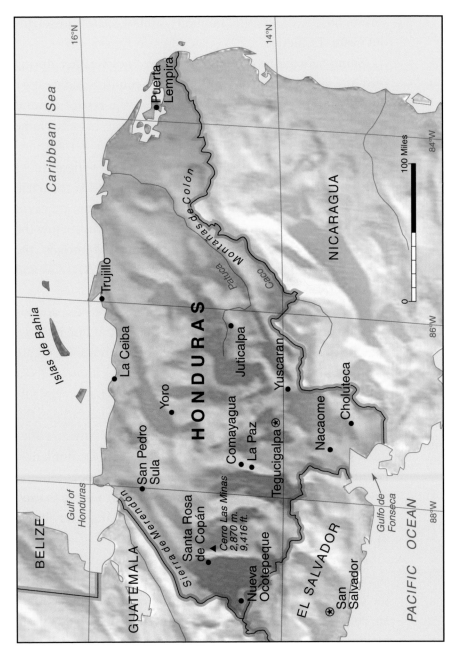

Approximately 81 percent of Honduras is composed of mountains, making much of the country's climate fairly temperate. The nation's highest point is Cerro Las Minas at 9,416 feet (2,870 meters) above sea level.

variations in temperature, humidity, and vegetation throughout Central America.

Some subregions of Honduras have cool weather during
certain seasons, and in other parts of the country cold weather
occurs routinely. As throughout much of the rest of Central
America, it is not seasonal shifts of sun angle that determine
these temperature changes, but rather differences in elevation.

Altitudinal life zones (life zones that change with altitude)
vary somewhat by latitude, although from Mexico to Brazil,
these zones have the same names. The four zones are *tierra
caliente, tierra templada, tierra fria,* and *tierra helado.* Only the
first three zones are found in Honduras. In tierra helado, the
"frozen land" higher than 12,000 feet (3,658 meters), snow and
ice appear year-round.

The *tierra caliente,* literally "hot land" or "hot earth," extends
from sea level at the shoreline up to 3,000 feet (1,000 meters).
In these coastal areas, year-round sunlight and humidity create
a consistently warm, and usually very wet, environment. As in
other parts of Central America, Honduras's plantation agriculture was traditionally practiced in this zone, particularly on the
northern coast. As in other Central American countries, settlement came late to the lowlands, which are, literally, hot lands.
Honduras's tierra caliente was very lightly populated until the
development of banana plantations in the early twentieth century. Early settlers made their way up into the cooler elevations
of the interior mountains.

In the "tempered land," the *tierra templada,* temperatures
are more moderate. At 3,000–6,000 feet (1,000–2,000 meters),
the templada is warm year-round, although cool temperatures
are common at night. At this elevation, corn and wheat can be
grown for subsistence, although coffee is the traditional commercial crop. Most Hondurans live in this zone.

The third zone, *tierra fria,* or cold land, extends up from
6,000 feet (2,000 meters) to the tree line, about 12,000 feet
(3,656 meters). Honduras's highest point lies within this zone.

Cerro Las Minas, in Celaque National Park, is 9,416 feet (2,870 meters) above sea level. The tierra fria is sparsely inhabited in Honduras, although a few small mountain villages may be found clinging to the frosty higher elevations.

Complicating the climate profile somewhat are the local names for the wet and dry seasons that characterize portions of the highlands and the Pacific lowlands. As in other parts of Central America, the dry season, from November to April, is known locally as "summer." The rainy season, from May to September, is called "winter."

Topography creates a diverse climate in a relatively small territory. In terms of physical surface features, the country may be divided into three distinct regions: the Caribbean lowlands and Bay Islands, the interior highlands, and the Pacific lowlands.

PHYSICAL REGIONS

The first region, the Caribbean lowlands, is known as the North Coast by many Hondurans. Three very different sections comprise this long shoreline. The middle section stretches a short distance east and west of the town of La Ceiba. Here, the mountains extend to within a few miles of the sea, and the coastal plain is narrow. To the east, the lowlands broaden, pushing inland along river valleys such as the Río Ulúa. This river is the industrial heartland of Honduras. Both Puerto Cortés, the country's largest port, and San Pedro Sula, the second-largest city in Honduras, are located here.

East of La Ceiba, the lowlands open out into an extensive area known as La Mosquitia, the Mosquito Coast. A place of mystery and legend, it is one of the largest wilderness areas remaining in Central America. Mosquitia is sparsely inhabited, unlike the developed western portion of the coast. Mangrove swamps, marshlands, pine savannahs, and tropical rain forests make travel difficult. Shallow brackish lagoons twist inland for miles. Archeologists have not fully explored most of its remote interior. According to one legend, the White City of the ancient

Mayans is located somewhere in the dense forests. Adding to the uniqueness of this subregion is the fact that it is home to the Miskito (also known as the Garifuna) and the Pech, people culturally distinct from other Hondurans. Rain falls year-round in the northern coastal plain, and Mosquitia averages the largest amounts—about 95 inches (2,400 millimeters). Annual amounts are slightly less at the western end of the coast, near San Pedro Sula. Unlike portions of the interior, there is no dry season or break from the consistently high temperatures and humidity. Occasionally, a *norte* (cold front) brings slightly cooler temperatures from the north.

The Islas de la Bahia (Bay Islands) lie a few miles off the northern coast. Small and relatively undeveloped, this string of islands parallels the shore from the central coast eastward to the Gulf of Honduras. Some of the bigger islands, such as Roatán, are being developed for tourism.

Interior highlands make up about 80 percent of the country's total land area. Many rivers have their headwaters in the interior. These streams drain the highlands and produce valleys with relatively fertile soils, such as the Valle de Sula. These are not the fertile volcanic soils typical of highland regions in Guatemala or Costa Rica, however. Vegetation in the higher elevations is varied. In some western portions, pine forests are dominant and are interspersed with oak and grassy mountain meadows. Some of the highest peaks in the country are here, notably Pico Congolón (about 8,200 feet, or 2,500 meters) and the Cerro Las Minas (9,416 feet, or 2,870 meters).

The central and western mountains contain silver and lead, and mining is an important industry in this region. Lago de Yojoa, the only natural lake of any size, also is located in the west-central part of the country. This lake is the country's largest source of freshwater, but it has been polluted by mining.

In contrast to the western mountains, eastern ranges tend to be covered with broadleaf evergreen forests. These mountains blend into Nicaragua and generally are not as rugged or as high as the western peaks. In a few remote eastern areas, remnants of rain forest are still found.

Deforestation is a problem in Honduras, as it is throughout Central America. Subsistence farmers use slash-and-burn techniques to create small farms in forested areas. Most tropical soils are poorly suited for sustainable agricultural production. Therefore, farmers must clear new plots every three to five years to maintain their subsistence lifestyles. Thus, forest lands are under constant pressure. Fires from slash-and-burn practices occasionally get out of control, creating wildfires that burn even more woodland.

Valley-scouring rivers are abundant in the highlands. Larger valleys provide sufficient grasslands and dry woodland to support livestock and, in some cases, commercial agriculture. The capital, Tegucigalpa, lies in one of these sheltered mountain valleys. At just under 3,280 feet (1,000 meters) in elevation, the city's climate is agreeable year-round (it has a relatively narrow temperature range). High temperatures in the warmest month average 86°F (30°C); in January, the coolest month, the average high is 77°F (25°C). The interior highlands also have a distinct dry season. Tegucigalpa, for example, typically receives only an inch or so of rain during the winter months. During spring and fall, rainfall is between 5 inches and 7 inches (127 to 178 millimeters) a month on average. As is characteristic of the tierra templada, temperatures in this region decrease as elevation increases.

The smallest physical region of Honduras is the Pacific lowlands, a strip of land averaging only 15–16 miles (25 kilometers) wide on the north shore of the Gulf of Fonseca. This area has the same year-round high temperatures as the northern coast. Unlike the Caribbean side of the country, though, it experiences a distinct dry season from November to May.

Near the gulf, the land is flat and swampy and is composed mostly of alluvial (stream-deposited) soils washed down from the mountains. Here the Choluteca River winds down from the

Located on Honduras's southern border, the coastal region around the Gulf of Fonseca is defined by its flat swampy land. The small village of Guapanile is typical of coastal communities in this region, where mangrove forests dominate the landscape.

highlands to Chismuya Bay on the gulf's eastern shores. This short coastline is indented, with winding lagoons and dense mangrove swamps, similar to those found in Mosquitia. These visually striking landscapes are formed by salt-tolerant plants that have adapted to life along the shoreline. Mangroves grow thick root assemblages that often extend above the water line. They create a hospitable environment for smaller plants as well as for birds and fish. Just under the surface, dense networks of mangrove roots provide safe breeding areas for shrimp and shellfish.

Honduras shares the waters of the gulf with El Salvador and Nicaragua, although two of the biggest islands belong to Honduras. Zacate Grande and El Tigre are ancient volcanic islands, part of the "Ring of Fire." These two extinct volcanic cones stand more than 2,300 feet (700 meters) above the gulf waters. Historically, they were navigational landmarks for ships entering the Pacific port of San Lorenzo.

FLORA AND FAUNA

Honduras lies at a point approximately midway through the narrow reach of land joining North and South America. This land bridge or isthmus was formed about 3 million years ago, during the late Pliocene epoch. It was a time that continents were taking on the shapes and arrangements that we know today. Earth's original land mass, called Pangaea, had long before broken apart into large thick portions, or plates. These plates drifted slowly atop the molten rock of Earth's interior. Sometimes the plates pull apart, sometimes they collide, and at other times, they buckle and shift. When they do, they create vast changes in surface features and also in aspects of the ocean bottoms. One such convulsive shift in the Caribbean plate created the land link between the North and South American continents. Over time, this dry passageway between north and south became a great corridor for migrating animals, plants, and eventually humans.

Through the millennia, a fascinating biological mosaic took shape here, as flora and fauna moved in both directions along the corridor of land. Biogeographers call this the Great American Interchange, a slowly unfolding ecological event that is still, in some ways, going on today. Dogs, cats, rodents, and bears from the Nearctic zoogeographic region of the northern latitudes moved south, colonizing new areas. Traveling from the opposite direction, opossums, armadillos, and porcupines came north from the Neotropical region south of the Tropic of Cancer, carving out new ecological niches. Likewise, plants moved in both directions, creating unique new landscapes of vegetation. South American grasses merged with pine trees from North America.

The isthmus acted like an ecologic filter, allowing some species to pass and blocking the transit of others. In this middle ground between north and south, many species, both plant and animal, reached their environmental limits. For example, Honduras's coniferous forests represent the southernmost extension of pines, as well as several other northern trees, including firs, cypress, juniper, and yew. Likewise, some southern animals, like the various New World monkeys, were stopped from pushing north by the Mexican plateau where the cool, dry environment barred their way.

Today, Honduras is home to an exotic array of tropical animals, both famous and little known. Jaguars, ocelots, and pumas are found in forest regions throughout the country. These mysterious members of the cat family conjure images of the primal wild. Another icon of tropical regions, the green iguana, lives in Mosquitia and other areas. White-faced monkeys and mantled howler monkeys with their long prehensile tails will surprise visitors with a range of startling cries and barks at sundown. The slow-moving and weirdly shaped sloth hangs high from tree branches and munches leaves. Sharing the forest canopy with the sloth is the kinkajou. This long-tailed tropical mammal is adapted to an arboreal life. On the floor of the forest, a relative of both the sloth and the armadillo has evolved a unique approach to eating. Toothless and shaggy-tailed, the giant anteater dines exclusively on ants and termites using its long, narrow snout and sticky tongue.

In all, more than 170 mammal species make their homes in Honduras. Some, such as wolves and armadillos, are found throughout Central America and parts of Northern America. Others, like tapirs, appear in Central and South America. A few other species are endemics (animals or plants found only in one region). One Honduran example is the Roatán Island agouti, a small burrowing rodent found nowhere else. A mainland endemic is the Honduran small-eared shrew, a small insect-eating mammal known for its poor eyesight and its tiny razor-sharp teeth. Shrews have some of the highest metabolism rates of any mammal in the world and must eat twice their own weight each day to survive. A mammal that probably evolved from a common ancestor of the shrew is the bat, the only mammal that can fly. Numerous bat species are found in Honduras.

They include the infamous vampire bat, which feeds entirely on blood, and one with a friendlier name, the fruit-eating bat.

With more than 700 bird species, Honduras is a bird watcher's paradise. Rare birds are a specialty. Some species, like the Harpy Eagle, are threatened by loss of habitat and are now protected by the government. One famous Central American bird—the resplendent quetzal—has been protected from hunting since ancient Mayan times. A traditional symbol of the Mayan people, the quetzal is a relatively small green, red, and white bird that sports iridescent green tail feathers up to 24 inches (60 centimeters) long. Quetzals are as highly prized today by photographers and ecotourists as they were during the Classic Mayan era. Unfortunately, the species is threatened by deforestation and habitat loss.

Three of the four major transregional migratory bird routes in the Western Hemisphere converge here. Honduras's forests, therefore, serve as wintering grounds for many migrating birds familiar to both North and South Americans.

Off the northern coast, a very different ecosystem is home to other threatened species. The Mesoamerican Reef extends about 450 miles (700 kilometers) from Mexico's Yucatán Peninsula along the coasts of Belize and Guatemala to the Honduran Bay Islands. It is the largest coral reef in the Western Hemisphere. Known as the Jewel of the Caribbean, this tropical habitat is home to 60 species of coral and numerous fish and mollusks. Scattered along the reef are atolls, the distinctive ring- or horseshoe-shaped coral structures that encircle lagoons. This fascinating ecoregion also includes the inshore waters, coastal wetlands, sea-grass beds, mangroves, and lagoons along the Caribbean shore and around the Bay Islands. The American manatee, the great aquatic mammal of seafaring myth, lives in the coastal waters between the reef and the mainland.

Five species of sea turtles swim and sometimes nest along the Honduran coast. The leatherback, loggerhead, hawksbill, Kemp's ridley, and green turtle are all endangered. These seagoing giants

At 450 miles (700 kilometers), the Mesoamerican Reef is the second-largest coral reef in the world behind Australia's Great Barrier Reef. The reef is pictured here just off the coast of Roatán, the largest of Honduras's Bay Islands.

spend most of their life in the water but return to the beach where they were born to lay eggs. Coastal development and commercial fishing have contributed to a sharp decline in their populations. Another large aquatic reptile, the American crocodile, shares these waters and also shares with the manatee a mythic reputation. The crocodile prefers salt marshes along the coast where it eats crabs, crayfish, birds, and turtles, but occasionally it swims out to sea for fish.

This entire ecoregion is threatened, although a principal threat—hurricanes—is beyond regulation. Other causes of concern, however, are within the control of people and governments and are being addressed. Environmental planning is relatively new to Honduras, but the government is making progress: It is working with international environmental groups and has identified threats to the country's rich biodiversity. New tourist developments along the coast and on the islands are being scrutinized more carefully before being approved. Nonpoint source pollution from agriculture has been another target of recent studies. Commercial overfishing and the threat of oil spills are other serious problems that planners are studying.

To protect the Mesoamerican Reef, the Honduran government is working with its neighbors, as well as with international environmental organizations. The MAR (Mesoamerican Reef) initiative is a broad-based plan to manage the fragile resources of the reef and the associated onshore ecosystems. Threatened species are a particular concern, especially the corals that created the reef and are highly vulnerable to pollution. Other intergovernmental conservation plans look at coastal and marine management along the Mosquito Coast and the Gulf of Fonseca. All these plans are examples of cross-border cooperation that is becoming common around the world.

Costa Rica is a Central American leader in environmental protection. Protecting biodiversity has created a strong ecotourist economy for that country. Honduras, although it lags far behind Costa Rica, has begun taking protection and conservation of its environmental resources seriously. So far, the government has set aside about 4.7 percent of the country's land area for protection. Some areas are protected as biorefuges. One example is the Cuero y Salado Wildlife Refuge, located on the northern coast just a few miles west of La Ceiba. This refuge is part of international planning for the coastal zones adjacent to the Mesoamerican Reef. It provides sanctuary for manatees, crocodiles, and monkeys. Other areas are designated as national parks. The largest is Río Plátano Biosphere Reserve, which holds more than 1.2 million acres (525,000 hectares). This park extends from the Mosquito Coast inland to the eastern mountains and encompasses mangroves, wetlands, savannahs, and mountain ecosystems. The crown jewel of Honduran parks, Río Plátano was designated a UNESCO World Patrimony site in 1982 in recognition of the global significance of its biodiversity. (UNESCO is the United Nations Educational, Scientific, and Cultural Organization.) Among other treasures, the park contains Honduras's last major tract of undisturbed tropical rain forest.

Also called equatorial forests, tropical rain forests are found worldwide between the latitudinal designations of the Tropic of Cancer and the Tropic of Capricorn. Like the popular image of the tropics as a place of constant heat and humidity, the popular image of the rain forest is also somewhat erroneous. It is typically not a jungle of dense vegetation, but rather a high canopied forest with dense growth overhead and a generally open forest floor with little undergrowth. Less than one percent of the light reaching the upper canopy finally reaches the forest floor. Therefore, only specialized plants can grow in the deep shadows of the thickly interwoven vegetation overhead. Life is concentrated high above the forest floor, in the microhabitats provided by the big trees. The branches and leaves are home to thousands of insect species, arboreal mammals such as sloths and monkeys, and dozens of different birds. Interlacing this complex biomass are many smaller epiphytic plants (growing on other plants) and vines that create a soft, flowing visual effect in the umbrella-like canopy.

The epiphyte family includes bromeliads, ferns, orchids, lichens, and other species that depend on other plants as platforms on which to hang or otherwise position themselves. Epiphytes are not parasites, though. They do not take nutrients from their hosts; rather, they use them only for support. With specialized hairlike growths called trichomes, epiphytes absorb nutrients and moisture from the air. Woody vines, or lianas, are another species adapted to compete in the vertically arranged ecosystem of the rain forest. Rooted in the forest's thin soil, lianas grow to enormous heights up into the highest reaches of the canopy. There, they support epiphytes and provide homes for mammals and birds.

Honduran rain forests, even those protected by national park or refuge status, are threatened by illegal logging, slash-and-burn agriculture, and the encroachment of (gradual takeover by) cattle ranchers. Other forest types are also threatened. The Mesoamerican pine-oak forest, one of the richest subtropical conifer forests in the world, stretches from southern Mexico through Honduras to Nicaragua. Although visually very different from the rain forest, the pine-oak forest is also high in biodiversity. Trees familiar to North Americans—pine, oak, sweet gum, and others—may be found here along with more exotic trees such as the guapinol or "stinking toe" tree.

Recent efforts to conserve and protect Honduran forests and the rich coastal, marine, and savannah ecosystems focus on educating local communities. People must take an active role in caring for their environments. This approach is slowly gaining momentum, with backing from international organizations and from the government. The people of Honduras know that environmental protection demands planning, persistence, and patience. Some threats to the country, however, cannot be stopped.

NATURAL HAZARDS

Earthquakes are common in Honduras, but when they occur they tend not to be as severe as those experienced in El Salvador or Nicaragua. The most serious natural hazard the country faces originates over the open waters of the east, rather than from underground.

Honduras lies within the hurricane belt. The West Indies, Atlantic and Gulf coasts of the United States, and the eastern coasts of Mexico, Belize, Guatemala, Honduras, and Nicaragua are all subject to tropical cyclones during certain times of the year. Cyclones are rotating air masses centered on an area of low pressure and are known by other names around the world (*typhoon* in the China Sea, *cyclone* in the Bay of Bengal and the southern Indian Ocean, and *willy-willy* in Australia). Hurricane season in Honduras runs from June to November when atmospheric and oceanic conditions are favorable for formation of tropical low pressure. For storms to grow, two things must happen: (1) Very warm water must be at the surface, which increases evaporation rates, and (2) the upper atmosphere must be experiencing high pressure; this acts as a cap on the development of the low pressure at the surface. When these conditions are right, hurricanes can grow to become the world's most destructive large storms.

Hurricanes form in the warm waters of the northern tropics, usually 15 to 25 degrees north latitude in the Atlantic Ocean, Caribbean Sea, or Gulf of Mexico. They often appear as areas of low pressure off the western coast of Africa near the Cape Verde Islands. Under the influence of the northeast trade winds, they move slowly westward until the midlatitude prevailing westerly winds deflect them in a curving path to the northeast. Sometimes this turn to the northeast begins far out over the ocean so that the storm curves back over the Atlantic, thus posing no threat to land. Frequently, however, atmospheric conditions lead hurricanes directly into Central America or the United States.

Although hurricanes do occur in the Pacific Ocean and occasionally affect Honduras from the west, Pacific storms tend to be much less severe. Honduras has been hit from the east by large storms that often destroy crops and kill people. Hurricane Francelia in 1969 and Hurricane Fifi in 1974 were two of the deadliest in recent memory. By far the worst in Honduran history, though, was the one that hit late in the season in 1998.

In mid-October, meteorologists began tracking a weak low pressure system as it moved off Africa's west coast. This system followed the routine path of such disturbances, slowly crossing the Atlantic and entering the Caribbean Sea. Slowly strengthening, it drifted west and intensified to tropical storm strength on October 22. Now it had a name, "Mitch."

Over the warm waters south of Jamaica, it grew to hurricane strength on October 24. Growing quickly into a Category 5 hurricane, the strongest on the Saffir-Simpson Hurricane Scale, Mitch entered the history books even before it neared the coast of Central America. A hurricane's intensity is measured by its central low pressure. This low pressure creates the two effects commonly associated with hurricanes—high winds and storm surge. Mitch achieved a central low pressure of 905 millibars and wind speeds of more than 170 miles (274 kilometers) an hour, becoming the largest October hurricane and the fourth-strongest storm in history, up to that point.

Mitch weakened as it neared the coastal waters off Honduras and came ashore as a Category 1 storm about 80 miles (128.7 kilometers) east of La Ceiba. Long before the eye crossed the beach, however, the rain had already begun far inland. It was Mitch's rain that people remember. As the storm moved inland, one of the developments most feared by hurricane watchers occurred. Its horizontal movement slowed to less than 5 miles an hour (8 kilometers/hour). As Mitch twisted its way into the heart of Honduras, it pulled supersaturated air into the highlands of Central America. The storm moved inland and turned south. Striking the capital city, it then headed west, following the mountains, and moved into Guatemala. Over the next three days, Mitch dumped torrents of water over the hills and mountains of Honduras, Guatemala, Nicaragua, and El Salvador. Some weather stations measured 48 inches (1,220 millimeters) of rain in less than 48 hours.

Rain fell throughout the Central American highlands where, that spring, wildfires had burned tens of thousands of acres. Denuded of vegetation, the bare hillsides and mountain slopes were particularly vulnerable to the deluge. The Choluteca, Ulúa, Lean, and other rivers became swollen torrents. Farms and entire villages were drowned or swept away. Along with the river flooding, mudflows and debris landslides destroyed thousands of houses. Twenty-five villages were completely destroyed. Maps of Honduras became useless, since most of the roads, bridges, and railroads were destroyed, and many villages had literally disappeared.

Mitch was the second-deadliest storm ever to strike Central America. The official toll of fatalities was more than 7,000. About 75 percent of the country's transportation infrastructure was destroyed. Ninety percent of the banana crop was ruined, and the country's other commercial crops suffered as well. In all, Honduras lost more than $900 million worth of agricultural production.

In addition, because of Mitch, coastal ecosystems on both sides of the country were altered. Mangrove forests on the Bay Islands were heavily damaged. Coral flats and sea-grass beds on the northern coast were damaged, hurting the shrimp aquaculture and other coastal fisheries. On the Pacific side, Río Choluteca flooded shrimp ponds and deposited a thick coat of silt through the mangrove forests.

In the spring of 1999, the World Meteorological Organization removed the name Mitch from its list of storm names, a memorial to one of the worst hurricanes in Honduran history.

3

Honduras Through Time

Christopher Columbus was the first known European to sail the Caribbean shores of Honduras. On his fourth and final voyage to the New World in 1502–1504, he found a land that already had an ancient history. The rise and fall of the Classic Mayan civilization had occurred centuries before. New people had migrated into the region from Mexico in the north and from the south. Great ceremonial cities such as Copán in western Honduras were abandoned and soon swallowed by dense rain forest vegetation. The people living in the forest had no understanding of the writing system devised by Mayan priests. The history, astronomy, and elaborate mathematical system of the Maya were soon forgotten.

Columbus was searching for a sea route through the great land mass that blocked his way to Asia, a route that did not exist. Although he had been disappointed on previous voyages, he persisted in his belief that a westward sea course to the Orient would be found, and he sailed south along the Central American coast looking for it. Accompanying him was his son, Fernando, who wrote a detailed account of the journey and chronicled the first encounter between Europeans and the people of Honduras.

Sailing along the Bay of Honduras past the Bay Islands, Columbus encountered a large trading canoe and seized it along with several men who were probably Mayans. The men provided Columbus with information about the coastline and the people living there. At Trujillo, on the central coast, Columbus stopped briefly to search for freshwater and more information. No other people were found, however, and he did not take time to explore the interior. Focused on his sea route exploration, he released the Mayans and continued sailing south before giving up his quest and returning to his base in the Caribbean. The next year, Columbus sailed for home still believing in the passage to Asia.

MAYA

The ancient Mayan civilization went through several distinct periods of expansion and decline. By the time of Columbus, the great achievements associated with the height of that civilization, the Middle Classic period, had been lost. The Mayans Columbus encountered were living in the aftermath of one of history's most mysterious collapses.

Mayan Timeline

A.D. 250 to A.D. 600	Early Classic
A.D. 600 to A.D. 900	Late Classic
A.D. 900 to A.D. 1500	Post-Classic

From its culture hearth in the lowlands of Mesoamerica, Mayan civilization spread over a wide territory. By the Early Classic period, it included the Yucatán Peninsula; the mountains and Petén region of Guatemala, Tabasco, and Chiapas in Mexico; and western Honduras.

Mayan control over these lands was never absolute. Much like the classic Greeks, the Maya were organized into small semi-independent city-states. Each of the major subregions competed with its neighbors for control of trade routes and for religious prestige. United by a common culture, these cities nevertheless developed their own dialects and variations on the common language, called Proto-Mayan. Today, the Maya speak more than two dozen languages that developed from this ancient mother tongue.

Likewise, Mayan religion developed subregional variations in the bigger city-states. Powerful ceremonial centers arose where priests ruled over a highly stratified society. Farmers, artisans, and warriors made up the three main classes in this society. Tikal in the Petén, Palenque in the Yucatan, and Copán in Honduras were three of the most powerful of these centers. Located near the present-day border with Guatemala, Copán was the largest city in the easternmost portion of the Mayan region. During the Classic period, it became a leading center of Mayan astronomy.

At Copán, the Mayans refined their solar-year calendar. The reckoning of time was essential to the underpinnings of Mayan religion. Astronomers at Copán created an elaborate system in which the year's 365 days were divided into 18 periods of 20 days each, plus 5 remaining days. They worked to perfect this system for centuries, eventually creating a calendar more accurate than the one we use today. The secrets of their complex system, based on intervals of 20, were guarded by the priestly caste. Mayan astronomers and mathematicians may have been the first people to have developed the concept of zero.

During the Classic period, the Maya were the undisputed masters of their domain. The rulers of Copán and the other centers of Classic Mayan culture were considered intermediaries between life on Earth and the spirit world. They held absolute power over the growing populations of the region. The flat-topped pyramids, ball courts, and other ceremonial structures

The Mayan Empire once stretched from present-day El Salvador in the south to Mexico's Yucatán Peninsula in the north. Located in western Honduras, Copán was one of the Mayas' most important cities, reaching its peak between the fifth and ninth centuries A.D.

that they built are wonders of the ancient world. Despite their achievements, Mayan engineers did not use the wheel, and iron-making was unknown to them. They decorated their buildings with intricate artwork—friezes, lintels, murals. Archaeologists have found a type of hieroglyphic script that is still being studied and translated today. One of the most elaborate hieroglyphic styles was created at Copán.

For reasons that will probably never be fully understood, the power of the priestly rulers suddenly declined in the ninth century. Copán and other ceremonial cities were abandoned, giving rise to the legend of the "Lost cities of the Mayans." The last hieroglyph at Copán is dated A.D. 800. Some scientists speculate that high population growth rates strained agricultural capacity. They believe that exhausted soils brought on ecological collapse and food shortages. Toltec invaders from Mexico took advantage of the weakened city-states and gained nominal control of much of the Mayan land. Although the priestly class disappeared, the Mayan people remained in place. Over the generations, however, they lost the ability to read the hieroglyphs and forgot the stories of their civilization's strange collapse.

Mayan civilization continued in diminished form in the Yucatán until the Spanish conquest. At the same time, distant groups related to the Maya migrated southward into the region. Various Toltec groups, such as the Chorotega, settled in the areas around Choluteca, in western and southern Honduras. In addition, Aztec people such as the Pipil moved into the mountains. Other indigenous peoples followed in waves of migration from the southern end of the isthmus. The Chibcha-speaking people settled in northeastern coastal areas. Related to peoples of Columbia and Panama, other migrants came from the south to settle eastern portions of the country: The Ulva, the Paya, the Sumu, and the Lenca were the most prominent. Linguists (language specialists) and other researchers are still studying the ancient connections and origins of these people. Separated by language, they were occasionally hostile to one another but nevertheless engaged in extensive trade throughout the Central American region. Unlike the Classic Maya, none of these people were city builders, living instead in small agricultural settlements. By the time of Columbus's voyages, the inhabitants of Honduras had diverse languages and cultures.

Columbus didn't explore the interior of the region, but he did name it. He called it Honduras, a name indicating the deep waters off the northern shore. He also named Guanaja, one of the Bay Islands, and Cabo Gracias a Dios, the eastern extremity of Honduras. A decade or so after Columbus returned to Spain, the Spanish came to Central America in force. They quickly subdued the native people and began to search for the riches they believed lay hidden in the dense forests and mountains.

THE SPANISH CONQUEST

At the time of Columbus's first voyage, the Spanish were engaged in the Reconquista, during which Christians reconquered that part of Europe. In 1492, the last of the Moors were driven out of the Iberian Peninsula after a centuries-long series of battles. The monarchy under Queen Isabella unified the Spanish state. One of the prime forces of this unification was Christianity. The Reconquista made Spain a militarily ambitious and confidant country. After Columbus's first voyage of discovery, the Spanish were poised to gain new territories and to spread the faith that had guided them through the Moorish wars. Just as Christianity gave them a common faith, the desire for riches gave them a common goal. At the forefront of the Spanish conquest of the New World were the conquistadors.

Despite overwhelming odds, the conquistadors conquered one region after another in the decades following Columbus's last voyage. Like falling dominoes, the Amerindian tribes gave way to them. Cortes defeated the Mexica, founded Mexico City in 1521, and moved south. His lieutenant, Pedro de Alvarado, conquered the Quiche and Cakchiquel Maya in Guatemala and founded Guatemala City in 1524. Cortes himself went to Honduras after a rebellion by one of his lieutenants and founded Trujillo in 1524. For the next 10 years, rival Spanish leaders fought each other as well as the native people.

In an attempt to stop the intermittent warfare, the Spanish divided Honduras into two districts, but fighting among tribes and rival Spanish continued. Alvarado returned from Guatemala to enforce a peace and to develop the gold mining industry. The demand for mine labor brought a few new settlers to the area. Much of the labor, however, came from Amerindian people, who were forced to work as virtual slaves. Conditions led to renewed resistance on the part of the natives. In 1537, a full-scale revolt broke out. It was led by Lempira, a Lenca leader, for whom the Honduran national currency was later named. Lempira successfully fought the Spanish for several years before he was murdered, and the revolt collapsed. After only 20 years in the New World, the Spanish had broken the military force of native people from Mexico to Peru.

The Spanish had iron-based weapons, which no people in the Western Hemisphere had seen before. Gunpowder weapons such as the harquebus were impressive and certainly intimidated people unfamiliar with firearms. Iron and steel swords and knives, iron helmets, and crossbows made the real difference in battle, however. Conquistadors also rode horses into combat and were accompanied by fiercely trained dogs. In addition to their technological edge, the Spanish enjoyed a significant advantage in their cultural approach to warfare. Ritual combat was common in Central America. Battles were fought between tribes, but few people were actually killed on the field. Captives were taken and some were later sacrificed in religious ceremonies or other public spectacles. In Europe, however, soldiers killed their enemies on the battlefield in large numbers, a practice that confused and terrified the Indians. The Spanish also were adept at exploiting existing rivalries between tribes and gaining the allegiance of some against the others.

Infectious diseases also favored the Spanish. Various European diseases were carried to the New World by the conquistadors, but few were as deadly to native peoples as smallpox. With no natural immunity, the native population fell into rapid decline during the early decades of the 1500s. Those natives who survived the epidemics faced food shortages and malnutrition. Their traditional agriculture was disrupted by the introduction and rapid spread of European livestock, especially cattle, into the lowlands. By 1540, only about 8,000 Amerindians remained in Honduras out of a population estimated to have been several hundred thousand before the conquest. Finally, while the native peoples were declining in numbers, the Spanish were colonizing their lands.

Spanish immigration to the New World was predominately male throughout the sixteenth and early seventeenth centuries. Family migration was encouraged but was considered too risky by most Spanish. In the sixteenth century, about 240,000 Spanish came to Mexico, Central America, and regions south. In the first half of the seventeenth century, another 195,000 immigrated, most from Andalusia and Castile. With a chronic shortage of Spanish women in the colonies, many men took Amerindian wives, and the result was a rapidly growing mestizo population. Mestizos are people of mixed Spanish and Amerindian heritage. The population of the New World began to rebound quickly from the early decades of the conquest as the mestizo birthrate far surpassed that of the remaining native people.

THE COLONIAL ERA

After the chaos of the conquest, Spanish colonial rulers imposed a rigid land system on the few native people left. This system was to have a lasting effect on the colony. Although formally abolished in the eighteenth century, its effects persist in some ways into the twenty-first century. The *encomienda* system placed native people and their lands under the direct control of local Spanish settlers. All the Spanish had to do was to provide religious instruction to the Amerindians and collect payments from them in the name of the Spanish Crown. Natives of each encomienda supplied labor for a certain number of days each year. In some areas of Latin America, this meant that they worked in the gold or silver mines. In others, they worked to produce crops for the Spanish. Reforms of the system gradually reduced the authoritarian control over the natives. By the time of Central American independence, the colonial land tenure system was abolished, but the cultural damage had been done.

Most of the population in Honduras and other newly independent countries in Central America were landless people, comparable to the peasants of medieval Europe or the serfs of Russia.

In the 1540s, Spanish settlement expanded and economic activity began to generate wealth. Cattle ranching and, for a time, the harvesting of sarsaparilla root became major industries. Gold and silver mining continued to dominate the economy, however. The mining centers established by Alvarado were located near the Guatemalan border, around the town of Gracias. In the early 1540s, the most intense mining activity shifted east to the Río Guayape Valley. Silver was also discovered in the east, and Gracias declined in economic and political importance. Other gold deposits were found near San Pedro Sula and the port of Trujillo. In the midst of the rapid expansion of the mining industry, Comayagua became the center of colonial Honduras. To meet the sudden increase in labor demands, the Spanish introduced African slaves into Honduras. By 1545, the province may have had as many as 2,000 slaves.

This period was characterized by intense interregional rivalry among the Spanish governors and the military over control of the mines. In 1544, the regional *audiencia* was established at Gracias. The audiencia was a Spanish governmental unit that combined both judicial and legislative functions. The audiencia presidents held the titles of governor and captain general and had almost complete power over people and resources in the colony. Despite its growing wealth from mining, Honduras could not compete politically with the more populous Spanish centers elsewhere in Central America. In 1549, the audiencia at Gracias was moved to Antigua, Guatemala. The subordination of Honduras to the captaincy general of Guatemala would remain until independence, almost 300 years later.

By the late sixteenth century, the gold and silver mines of Honduras had declined in production. As a result, the colony

Founded in 1537, the Spanish settlement of Comayagua served as the capital of the Honduras District in the province of New Spain during the colonial period. The town is depicted here in this mid-nineteenth-century sketching.

had become an economically depressed and largely forgotten remnant of the Spanish Empire. Some mining continued, but the larger mines of Mexico and South America far overshadowed them in generating wealth for the Spanish. After some modest attempts to create an export farm economy failed, most mestizos and Amerindians were subsistence farmers. Town development slowed as survival for most Hondurans meant living off the land in dispersed farms in the countryside. Cattle ranches that produced beef for the Guatemalan market were established in some lowland areas. This small export activity employed few people, however, and did not result in further economic growth.

The Bourbon Dynasty replaced the Habsburgs on the throne of Spain in 1700, and the new rulers set out to make their New World Empire more profitable. Bourbons introduced reforms aimed at eliminating colonial corruption and encouraging development. For the next 100 years, Spain was locked in intense competition with France and England for control over lands and resources in the Western Hemisphere.

Defending the New World Empire against invasion became a priority for the Bourbon rulers. For many years, English pirates had attacked Honduras's Caribbean coast. The port of Trujillo, site of Columbus's landing, was sacked and burned by pirates in 1643 and was abandoned by the Spanish for almost a century. Although privateers raided coastal settlements and scuttled Spanish ships, they also attempted to plant colonies along the Caribbean coast and in the Bay Islands. British traders and ex-pirates who intermarried with freed black slaves began to come to the Bay Islands in the eighteenth century. For the most part English speaking, these British and Afro-Caribbean people found little Spanish presence and quickly came to dominate the islands.

In addition to the de facto colonies in the islands, the British planted small settlements on the mainland coast at Cabo Gracias a Dios and to the west at the mouth of the Río Sico. In these out-of-the-way locations far from Spanish control, the mixed British-African towns flourished. Río Sico's population reached almost 4,000 by the mid-eighteenth century.

The British created another type of problem in Honduras by encouraging Mosquito Coast peoples to resist Spanish control. The region known as La Mosquitia was one of the largest wilderness areas in colonial Honduras. It became a haven for escaped slaves who found refuge with small numbers of Amerindians who had remained outside the Spanish sphere of influence. Freed Caribbean slaves and a small population of British traders, pirates, and others who sought freedom from both English and Spanish law also hid out in the vast wilderness. Intermarriage among these groups produced the unique culture of the Miskitos.

Under the Bourbons, the Spanish decided to retake the coastal areas Britain had stolen from them. They rebuilt Trujillo in 1780 as a military base to use for control of the coast, and a few years later, they regained the Bay Islands. As the competition between Spain and Britain began to wind down in the late eighteenth century, internal Honduran political conflicts began to dominate the colony's life. The term *creole* was used to describe children born in the colonies of Spanish parents. This was to distinguish them from the mestizos, who made up the larger share of the population.

Creole families became a powerful political force just before the turn of the nineteenth century. They wanted free trade, an end to the Spanish monopolies in Honduras, and a representative government like the one they saw taking shape in North America. Creoles also saw the British colonies shaking free of European control, and they wanted the same thing for Spain's Central American colonies. They also wanted an end to the domination of the church in local judicial and political matters.

Back in Europe, Spain unwisely allied itself with Napoleon, who brought about war by forcing the Spanish king to abdicate in 1808. With political revolt at the center of the empire, many colonists took advantage of the chaos to press ahead with their plans for independence. As Spain's hold over its colonies weakened throughout the early years of the century, a new struggle was emerging for control of Honduras.

INDEPENDENCE

On September 15, 1821, a junta (group of revolutionaries) made up of leaders from Honduras, El Salvador, and Guatemala convened in Guatemala City to declare independence from Spain. Some moderates and conservatives in the group favored a union with Mexico. Liberals favored an independent republican federation. The debate about the form of the new government continued for almost two years. However, in June 1823, the United Provinces of Central America (UPCA) was formed. Comprised of Guatemala, Honduras, El Salvador, Costa Rica, and Nicaragua, the UPCA was a league of independent states. Each of the five had its own national assembly and its own executive. The seat of the UPCA government was

De Eſpañol, y Meſtiſa; Caſtiſa.

During the colonial era, intermarriage was common between Spanish settlers and Amerindians. The couple's offspring were deemed mestizos, which today represent approximately 90 percent of Honduras's population.

established in Guatemala City. Much as the colonial Audiencia of Guatemala had dominated Honduras, the UPCA government came to represent Guatemalan control over the other four states in the league. Tensions in the organization polarized two groups—conservatives and liberals—who began a political struggle that would last into the twenty-first century.

One problem with Honduran and Central American politics today is that these political positions are not confined to any one state in the region. Liberals or conservatives in one country routinely interfere in the politics of their neighbors. Politics easily cuts across state boundaries in a region where everyone speaks the same language and shares the same colonial past. In the beginning of this regional ideological divide, conservatives were distinguished by several core issues. They were strongly prochurch and supported a Catholic Church monopoly over education. Traditional Spanish cultural and religious values were to be maintained by a strong centralized government. In addition, significantly, mestizos were not considered as political or social equals and were to be excluded from power.

Liberals wanted to limit church authority and to separate religious institutions from those of the government. The creation of an open political and economic system similar to that of the United States was their goal. On the issue of the place of mestizo and native people, liberals wanted them included in a mainstream national society, not relegated to the status of second-class citizens.

Liberal-conservative battles over the UPAC began soon after the organization was founded. The new constitution outlawed slavery but denied full citizenship rights to Indians and mestizos, much to the dissatisfaction of liberals. Struggles between the two groups led to a civil war in El Salvador from 1826 to 1829 and the election of the liberal Francisco Morazán as UPAC president in 1830. Morazán alienated many mestizos, the very people the liberals sought to help, by confiscating church lands and abolishing the church's independent court system. A peasant revolt led by Rafael Carrera, a mestizo, defeated Morazán in 1838. With the UPAC in shreds, Honduras declared independence on November 15, 1838, and two months later formally adopted its own national constitution.

Despite its nominal independence from the other Central American republics, Honduras was buffeted by the winds of interregional politics for the rest of the century. Following the breakup of the UPAC, a tightly connected group of conservatives ruled Honduras, as well as Guatemala and El Salvador. Allied with the church, they controlled the region for most of the next 30 years. Numerous coups and small-scale civil wars kept the region from developing economically. The British took advantage of the chaos to regain control over the Bay Islands in the 1830s, although they returned the islands and a portion of La Mosquitia to Honduras in 1860.

In 1865, a new constitution established the Republic of Honduras. A brief period of relative stability was shattered by another civil war between liberals and conservatives that lasted from 1872 until 1876. At the conclusion of this war, the liberals gained most political power and began to open the country to foreign investment.

BANANAS AND U.S. INVOLVEMENT

By the last decades of the nineteenth century, trade with North America began to shape Honduran politics as much as regional Central American politics had. The weak national economy was based on extractive industries. Mining had been revitalized by investment from the United States, and although profits from gold and silver were significant, relatively few jobs were created. Other than mining, foreign investment was in coffee, sugarcane, and banana plantations. The plantation system created a demand for workers, but wages were low.

In 1880, most of Honduras's 382,000 people continued to live as subsistence farmers. Honduras had few schools and no public libraries or newspapers. Never politically stable, the country experienced numerous regime changes and insurrections. Despite calling itself a representative government, Honduras was a dictatorship. The waning years of the nineteenth century brought vast changes, however, as the national economy became dependent on one export crop—bananas.

In 1889, the business later known as the Standard Fruit Company began to ship bananas from Honduras to the port of New Orleans. The U.S. banana industry grew rapidly. As supplies to North American markets became steady, residents quickly developed a taste for what had previously been a rare and exotic item. Governments of the five Central American republics—Honduras, Guatemala, El Salvador, Nicaragua, and Costa Rica—became locked in an economic embrace with foreign-owned banana companies. The companies, in turn, squeezed enormous concessions from them. The derisive term *Banana Republic* was applied to Honduras and other Central and South American states dependent on banana exports.

The United States developed closer trade and investment relationships with Central America. As the banana and coffee markets came to be dominated by U.S. companies, the U.S. government came to view the region in a new light. The last vestiges of the colonial Spanish Empire in the Western Hemisphere were gone with the conclusion of the Spanish-American War in 1898. The United States now saw the Caribbean basin as being within its exclusive sphere of influence. Soon, the country decided to build a canal linking the Pacific and Atlantic oceans through the Central American country of Panama. This huge project focused more attention on the region and gave the United States an additional reason to support stability and development.

Beginning early in the new century, the United States established a pattern of intervention in the region that was to last for decades. In 1907, after Nicaraguan forces invaded Honduras in an attempt to oust the president, the United States landed troops on the Caribbean coast. The U.S. Navy protected the Honduran president's stronghold from the invaders. After the fighting ceased, the United States called a regional meeting of the five Central American presidents in 1908. New peace treaties were signed, promising agreements on neutrality and cooperation, but other than talk and meaningless promises, little was accomplished.

For the first 20 years of banana exportation, Honduran growers controlled on-site management and production, whereas the U.S. companies controlled shipping and distribution. By 1913, production and management of the plantations came under the direct administration of the foreigners who began interfering in Honduran politics.

As the United States came to be perceived as Central America's police force, competition among international banana and other fruit companies became fierce. The arrival of new banana companies in Honduras introduced new levels of intrigue and new opportunities for political conflict. The United Fruit Company entered the country in 1910 and received enormous land subsidies from the government. Honduran leaders believed the railroad companies that were subsidiaries of United Fruit would create a national rail system that would benefit the entire country. What happened, however, was that the company used the virtually free land to open up new areas to plantation development. Within a few years, United Fruit controlled almost all of the suitable plantation land along the Caribbean coast. Coastal cities such as La Ceiba and Trujillo, as well as inland towns such as El Progreso and La Lima, became company towns whose fortunes were directed by the foreigners.

Rapid development of the banana industry sparked the beginning of a labor movement in Honduras that resulted in major strikes. The first occurred in 1917 and 1918. Tensions brought on by the strikes and labor demands led to another revolution in 1919. U.S. Marines were sent in as peacemakers, and a truce was mediated, but the strikes continued. In 1920, a general strike hit the Caribbean coast, temporarily shutting down almost all of the banana production in the country.

In the midst of widespread labor unrest and increased U.S. influence in the region, the Central American republics again attempted to create a regional government. On January 19, 1921, the Pact of Union among Honduras, Guatemala, Costa Rica, and El Salvador was signed, creating the Federation of Central America. A provisional federal council was organized, and a federal constitution was written. In December of 1921, though, a revolution in Guatemala successfully brought the new arrangement to an end before it really had a chance to begin. The federation was dissolved officially on January 29, 1922. Unfortunately, the short-lived union did nothing but renew old disagreements over borders between the five republics. Several of these border disputes have simmered along in Central American politics ever since.

The most threatening border issue was between Honduras and Nicaragua. To settle the dispute, the United States organized a conference of Central American presidents in December 1922. Under the guidance of U.S. negotiators, a treaty of neutrality was written and a Central American court of justice was planned. Measures were drawn up to limit armaments and to advance economic development in the region. The various treaties and agreements were ratified by the participants in 1923, but little was done to put them into effect.

The following year, a frustrated candidate for the Honduran presidency established another dictatorship. This sparked yet another war between conservative and liberal interests. In what had become an unfortunate pattern in Honduras and Central America, the United States once again sent in troops to protect U.S. business investments. The Honduran dictator was killed in the fighting, and the United States backed a peace agreement among the contending forces. One of the main objectives of the agreement was to stop insurgents from using bases in neighboring countries, a common tactic of Central American revolutionaries for decades. The old division between liberals and conservatives now had a new international dimension, as the United States intervened routinely to quell outbreaks of violence. The repeated interventions, however, like the well-meaning agreements, led to no long-term solutions. The basic problems of poverty, illiteracy, foreign ownership, and political corruption continued.

By 1930, Honduras was producing one-third of the world's bananas. A merger between United Fruit and its leading competitor in Honduras created a monolithic plantation production system, but the Great Depression ruined any promise of a more stable banana industry. As the U.S. economy crashed in the early 1930s, banana exports declined sharply. Thousands of plantation workers lost their jobs. In the middle of this dire economic downturn, epidemic outbreaks of fungus and leaf blight struck. Thousands of acres of plantation land were affected, which resulted in even more jobs lost. Within two years, the banana diseases were under control, but by then much of the industry had shifted its production to other countries unaffected by the blight. The United Fruit Company lost some of its direct control over Honduran lands and workers. Nonetheless, it remained the largest landowner in the country and continued to play a central role in Honduran politics throughout the rest of the century.

Perhaps the greatest intrigue involving United Fruit and other banana companies came in the 1950s with explosive consequences for Honduras and Guatemala. Guatemala had elected a leftist president, Jacobo Arbenz, who wanted to take over banana company lands. Many of his political opponents were exiled to Honduras. Consequently, under the influence of United Fruit's powerful Washington, D.C., lobby, the United States began to pressure Honduras to assist in overthrowing the Arbenz government. Part of the U.S. strategy involved a disinformation program aimed at bolstering Honduran support for a war against Arbenz. After United Fruit refused to pay dockworkers for overtime, a national strike paralyzed the country for more than two months. This strike was blamed, inaccurately, on Guatemala's leftists, but in fact Honduran banana workers had organized it. Meanwhile, the United States supplied Arbenz's opponents with arms and money, and Honduras was used as a staging area for the successful invasion of Guatemala. U.S.-backed forces quickly overthrew Arbenz, and the plantations were secured. In the aftermath of the invasion, Honduras signed an agreement allowing U.S. military exercises in Honduran territory. The national strike in Honduras was settled and workers gained the right to unionize, although strike leaders were arrested. Shortly after, the banana companies begin to mechanize, and hundreds of workers were laid off.

In the mid-1950s, two important events signaled a change in Honduran politics and society: In 1955, women were given the right to vote, and in October 1956, another coup was staged. This one was different, however. For the first time, a Honduran coup was carried out without bloodshed. The armed forces acted as a governmental body, not as a tool of a political party or an individual leader. The officers who led the coup were largely U.S.-trained professionals who had definite reformist goals for the new government. This newly professionalized Honduran military leadership would play a deciding role in Honduran politics for the next 40 years.

Regional Central American politics again threw the country into turmoil in 1969. Because of civil war in El Salvador, for several years, refugees had been streaming across the poorly defended border with Honduras. Honduran politicians blamed the approximately 300,000 refugees for poor wages and the high rates of unemployment that plagued the country. Honduras began to expel refugees, who reluctantly returned to El Salvador.

In the middle of heightened tensions between the two countries, the World Soccer Cup preliminaries were being

Honduran employees of the United Fruit Company organized the Great Banana Strike of 1954, which brought the banana industry to a standstill. More important, for Honduran workers, the event paved the way for the establishment of labor unions in the country. Today, Honduras is the most unionized nation in Central America.

held. In June, the national soccer teams of Honduras and El Salvador began a three-game elimination match series. Fighting among fans broke out during the first game in Tegucigalpa. During the second match in San Salvador, the fighting turned into widespread violence and rioting. Honduran fans were attacked savagely. In retaliation, Hondurans turned on Salvadoran refugees, attacking hundreds. Some were killed, and thousands of terrified refugees fled across the border into El Salvador. On June 27, diplomatic relations were broken, and both countries issued inflammatory attacks on each other. The war of words broke out into open hostilities on July 14. The Salvadoran army and air force attacked targets inside Honduras. After some initial confusion, the Honduran military regrouped and fought the invaders to a standstill. A cease-fire was arranged by the Organization of American States on July 18. El Salvador withdrew its forces early in August, and the infamous "Soccer War" was over.

The war was a disaster for both sides. Public opinion in Honduras condemned the military for their slow response to the invasion. Trade between the two countries was disrupted for years, and the border area was militarized. Almost 2,000 people were killed; most were Honduran civilians. Thousands of people in both countries were uprooted.

Throughout the 1970s, the pattern of coups and ever more repressive dictatorships continued. In 1975, the continuing political influence of the banana industry made international headlines with the "Bananagate" scandal. The United Brands Company was caught giving a $1.2 million bribe to the Honduran finance minister in exchange for canceling a proposed export tax on bananas. The political turmoil of "Bananagate" came just after one of the most destructive natural disasters in Honduran history. At the height of the 1974 storm season, Hurricane Fifi hit the Caribbean coast, devastating the banana plantations and killing about 10,000 people.

Interregional chaos continued into the 1980s as Honduras became an island of relative stability in a sea of revolutionary violence. On Honduras's southwestern border, El Salvador's cruel civil war produced thousands of refugees. On its eastern flank, Honduras faced the Nicaraguan revolution and its costly aftermath, the Contra War. Thousands of Nicaraguan refugees fled the fighting between the Nicaraguan dictator, Anastasio Somoza Debayle, and the Sandinistas, who eventually overthrew him. Almost as soon as the Sandinistas took power, however, Somoza's backers began to fight the new government, which created another wave of refugees.

The United States viewed Honduras as the logical point from which to intervene in these two conflicts. U.S. strategy in the region had changed since the early twentieth century, however, when troop deployments to Central American hotspots were routine. Now the United States worked through regional governments. With Guatemala engaged in its own long-standing civil war, Honduras was the only functioning government with the capacity to help. The United States dramatically increased its military aid to Honduras, from $2 million in 1980 to $144 million in 1982–1983. With U.S. encouragement, eastern Honduras became a base for the anti-Sandinistas—the Contras—to invade Nicaragua. Honduran troops initially supported the Contra incursions into Nicaragua. Over time, however, the Contras wore out their welcome in Honduras. They committed atrocities in Honduras as well as in Nicaragua and alienated their early supporters, many of whom came to see them as a foreign army occupying their country. Anti-U.S. and anti-Contra sentiment became widespread in 1985. Honduras finally expelled the contras and began to seek its own solutions to the problems in El Salvador and Nicaragua.

Working with the governments of Costa Rica, Guatemala, El Salvador, and Nicaragua, Honduras signed the Arias Peace Plan in 1987. The plan, named for the Costa Rican president who masterminded the negotiations, was an attempt to stabilize the region. It called for democratic reforms, release of political prisoners, free elections, and an end to foreign assistance to insurgents. The Arias Plan was seen as the beginning of a new era for Central America, one in which the influence of both the Soviet Union, who had backed the Sandinistas, and the United States took a backseat to regional solutions and initiatives. Oscar Arias won the 1987 Nobel Peace Prize for finally bringing peace to the region.

By the late 1980s, regional politics began to stabilize and Honduran leaders began to focus on economic development. In 1990, the Honduran government imposed a free-market austerity program. Designed by the International Monetary Fund to restore fiscal credibility to impoverished and indebted states, the program caused some economic pain. Wages for most jobs were frozen. Some small businesses closed. Workers went on strike to protest wage cuts and the loss of jobs. The short-term disruptions were relatively minor, though, and led to gradual improvement of Honduras's international credit standing with the World Bank. Foreign investment began to trickle in.

In 1997, Carlos Roberto Flores of the Liberal Party was elected president. He quickly moved to diversify the economy and make government more efficient. He believed that standards of living could be improved only by attracting foreign investment. In an effort to move Honduras further along the path to a stable democracy, he also passed legislation giving control of military forces to a civilian minister of defense to be appointed by the president.

Before any of Flores's new initiatives could produce results, the 1998 hurricane season brought another record-breaking storm to Honduras. Hurricane Mitch rendered 2 million homeless, killed approximately 7,000 people, and almost completely destroyed Honduras's agricultural sector. The devastating storm also wiped out much of the transportation network.

The country still struggles to fully recover from Mitch. In 2000, a free-trade agreement signed between Mexico, Honduras, Guatemala, and El Salvador was popular in Honduras largely because it was seen as a way to stimulate the storm-battered economy.

During the first decade of the twenty-first century, Honduras has continued its democratic reforms, although not without sporadic political crises. The economy is still dependent on the primary sector—agricultural exports such as bananas, melons, and seafood. Free trade and increased foreign investment offer the greatest hope for the future. In the next chapter, we'll look at how the Honduran economy is developing on the world stage.

4

People
and Culture

National identity and ethnicity are difficult to pick apart in Honduras. In some parts of the world, these two ways of perceiving one's citizenship and one's individual identity are simply the same. Japan, for instance, is a nation-state. To be Japanese means to share citizenship and ethnocultural identity. To be a Honduran is a little more complicated. About 90 percent of Honduras's nearly 8 million people are mestizo, that is, people of mixed Amerindian and European ancestry. Mestizos are found throughout Middle and South America. In all of the Central American republics, they are the dominant ethnic group in terms of numbers. Regional variations in mestizo culture exist, but, for the most part, from place to place, mestizos are more alike than different. They are almost all Spanish-speaking Roman Catholics who share a similar Spanish colonial history. Social conventions and manners are derived from Spanish sources, so European visitors might find much that is familiar.

Because mestizo culture is a result of the blending of colonial and Amerindian people, however, the traditional sources have been modified and tempered by local customs.

Until recently, mestizos were treated as second-class citizens in Central America. Small groups of social elites, usually of European ancestry, controlled the governments and ran the economies. Honduras has been somewhat luckier than its neighbors in this regard. Class distinctions in Honduras have not been as volatile or divisive as in Guatemala or El Salvador. Mestizo culture is family oriented. In a country with a poorly developed economy, families are the key to survival.

POPULATION FIGURES

Even today, despite some progress in economic development, many Hondurans remain subsistence farmers. In a traditional culture, children contribute to the family's economic well-being, and because the country lacks a governmentally organized social safety net, large families represent a measure of security for the elderly. Most Hondurans maintain close relations with their extended families. Demographic data (population statistics) for Honduras are, for the most part, based upon educated guesses. The country's last official census was taken in 2001 (new data should appear in 2012, based upon the scheduled 2011 census). The mid-2010 population estimate is 7,989,415. Currently, this number increases by about 2 percent each year, nearly twice that of the world rate of about 1.1 percent annual gain. The total fertility rate (the average number of children a woman will have in her lifetime) for Honduras is 3.17, a rate that contributes to a growing population (2.1 is the replacement rate). As the country develops and educational and vocational opportunities for women improve, the fertility rate will decline. For now, the population is young and will remain so for some time. The median age is only 20.7 years, compared to 36.8 for the U.S. and 40.7 for Canada. Providing education, job-training, and employment for this young population will be an ongoing challenge for Honduras. About 80 percent of Honduran adults are literate, although most adults have not finished high school.

HONDURAN SOCIETY

Most Hondurans are somewhat formal and socially conservative. Even people of modest means display Old World manners inherited from the colonial era. As a result, Hondurans tend to be very polite and even charming in their day-to-day interactions with other people. Another part of this old colonial legacy involves a double standard for men and women, however. The patriarchal world of *machismo* is still very much alive. Machismo leads to rigid expectations about gender roles, family size, and even political behavior. Husbands or close male relatives are expected to lead women in most social or public situations. This is one of the reasons why many women find that professional training and political leadership are life choices that are still closed to them. As the Honduran economy begins to diversify slowly, and educational achievement becomes available to more women, this legacy will change. For many Hondurans, though, the change is slow in coming.

Religion

One aspect of Honduran culture that is changing rapidly is religion. The Spanish brought the Roman Catholic Church to Honduras in the early sixteenth century. And the Church has played a central role in the political and economic development of the country ever since. Today, the Catholic Church remains the largest faith in the country, although changes are under way. About 96 percent of the population is Catholic, and only 4 percent is Protestant, but evangelical missionaries are making rapid progress in converting Hondurans. Beginning in the 1980s and 1990s, Protestant groups have steadily attracted new members. Groups such as the Church of God, the Seventh Day Adventists, and the Methodists have invested much time

Approximately 96 percent of Hondurans are Roman Catholic, but church membership is declining as more Hondurans are turning to evangelical Protestant groups. Despite this shift, the Catholic influence remains strong; cathedrals such as Iglesia Los Dolores in the capital of Tegucigalpa represent the country's Spanish heritage.

and money in challenging the traditional Catholic hold over Central America. Much as the Spanish missionaries did centuries before, the evangelicals are bringing well-organized social service programs to impoverished Hondurans.

Much of the debate between the tradition-minded Catholic Church and the new missionaries focuses on the issue of national identity in the postcolonial world. This debate is played out in the media. Evangelicals have a newspaper, a radio station, and a new Internet TV channel that express their opinions on the religious establishment. The Catholics also have a television channel that broadcasts religious programming 24 hours a day. Evangelicals attack traditional Catholicism as a legacy of Spanish colonialism, part of the past that should be left behind as the country develops. According to some evangelicals, the traditional church never dealt with the problem of poverty. For evangelicals, poverty is a sign of weakness and insufficient faith. Many of them preach that proper spiritual guidance leads to material wealth and well-being. This is a powerful message for people who have been disenfranchised for generations. Roman Catholic leaders counter that evangelicals are dominated by U.S. groups associated with right-wing political agendas. Some think that following the spiritual path of the evangelicals will lead to the loss of Honduran identity and the Americanization of mestizo culture. So the arguments go back and forth.

The brand of Catholicism practiced in Honduras is conservative by North American standards. Saints are widely regarded as special protectors, and many people keep pictures or small statues of particular saints in their homes. The patron saint of Honduras is the Virgin of Suyapa. The Basilica of the Virgin, near Tegucigalpa, is believed to have miraculous powers. As a result, it is visited by thousands of people every year who seek cures for ailments and injuries.

Syncretism is also practiced, particularly in remote areas. A blending of different religious beliefs, syncretism is one way traditional Amerindian (and, in the case of the Garifuna, African) religious practices survive in otherwise Christian countries. In Honduras, for example, some people who consider themselves devout Catholics also visit shamans, traditional "faith healers." They consult seers for advice and buy charms and potions to control the behavior and the emotions of others. In some rural areas, many people still believe in witchcraft and routinely protect themselves from spells. For example, the "evil eye" is greatly feared by some people. They take precautions to guard themselves and especially their children from strangers who might have the power to harm them with a glance.

Religious traditions are rich in a country that has been predominately Catholic for more than 400 years. For many Catholics, Semana Santa, or Holy Week, is the culmination of the Christian year in Honduras. As in other Central American countries, unique processions mark Holy Week observances. The festivities begin with Palm Sunday processions, followed by others on Holy Tuesday, Good Friday, and Easter Sunday. Combining color, Spanish and Honduran symbolism, Catholic iconography, and music, Holy Week processions are distinct expressions of religious faith. In the capital city of Tegucigalpa, Holy Week participants number in the thousands, as fraternal church societies, civic organizations, school groups, and church officials parade solemnly to the sounds of muffled drums, traditional fifes and drums, and brass bands. On Easter Sunday, colored sawdust and flower petals are used to create elaborate *alfombras*. These are sawdust carpets depicting scenes from the life, death, and resurrection of Jesus, as well as other images relevant to the season. In the last few years, Holy Week has begun to attract tourists, subtly changing the community aspects of the observance.

Many of the Catholic structures in Honduras were built in the mid-sixteenth to the mid-eighteenth centuries. During this period in European church architecture, elaborate ornamentation was the style. Cathedrals in the bigger towns are imposing structures, with massive stone exteriors, elaborately carved wooden doors, and ornate altars. Interiors are decorated with statues and paintings of saints and biblical scenes. Smaller churches, monasteries, convents, and chapels were constructed by the thousands throughout Honduras and neighboring countries. Much of this architecture has been maintained or restored, lending a deep historic texture to the cultural landscape.

Language

Another key marker of cultural identity is language. As in religion, Honduras has a single dominant language, Spanish, that is nearly universal. This language will most certainly be the majority tongue for at least the foreseeable future. It is the language of education, government, and business. Almost all Hondurans speak it, and for the vast majority, it is their first language. Several Amerindian tongues are still spoken by people on the remote northeastern coast or in the isolated mountains of the interior. Because so few people speak them, they are among the many languages worldwide considered to be endangered. These languages, like the Chorotega, the Pipil, and the Hicaque, have only a few hundred or few thousand speakers at most. Most young people from these communities learn Spanish rather than the old tongues.

Honduras is also home to several distinct creole languages. Originally, the term *creole* was used in reference to children of French or Spanish colonists born in the New World. Later, it took on various other meanings, depending on where in the Western Hemisphere it was used. For linguists, the term indicates a language that has developed from mixed sources. A creole develops over time as a common language spoken between different linguistic groups engaged in trade or routine cross-cultural communication. Creoles are often situational languages that develop to fill a particular need at a particular time. Many of them do not last long, but some of these provisional local languages survive over time and develop the characteristics of distinct languages. Most retain strong elements of their sources and are identified in terms of their strongest constituent language. An example of the latter is the creole spoken by the population of the Bay Islands. Their language is an English-based creole sometimes referred to as Caribbean English. Most of the vocabulary is familiar to English speakers, although the cadence of the speech and the pronunciation of many words are unmistakably Caribbean.

Popular Culture

Contemporary "urban" popular culture in Honduras is much like that of other Central American countries. The Honduran diet is based on beans, rice, tortillas, fried plantains, meat, potatoes, cream, and cheese. American fast food is slowly changing some eating habits, as popular Northern American franchises spread to the larger cities, such as Tegucigalpa. Items such as French fries, hamburgers, and pizzas are increasingly found on the menus of cafés and restaurants.

Musical tastes are changing as well, as Northern American pop music is heard commonly on radio and television. Still, the most popular music in Honduras today is *cumbia*, a genre that is played enthusiastically throughout Central America and beyond. A blend of Spanish and African styles and rhythms, it resembles salsa in its energy and rhythmic complexity. Dancers find it a perfect style in which to individualize traditional Latin dance steps. More traditional types of music survive as well. Marimba music has long been popular throughout Honduras. An instrument of West African origin, it was brought to Central America by slaves in the sixteenth century and adopted by the mestizos. In the countryside, older wooden versions of the instrument may still be heard. In bigger towns, amplified marimbas accompanied by electric guitars and drums perform contemporary Honduran and U.S. pop tunes.

Ethnicity

Honduras is overwhelmingly a mestizo country, both in terms of population and in culture. Some ethnic diversity can be found there, however. Various indigenous people comprise 7 percent of the population; 2 percent is black, and 1 percent is European. These minority groups, with the possible exception of the Europeans, are assimilating into mestizo culture as the country modernizes.

One indigenous group that is slowly assimilating into mestizo culture is the largest native tribe in Honduras, the

Lenca. Numbering about 50,000, they live in remote villages in the mountainous western portion of the country. As more and more of their young people leave their traditions and language behind and cross over into mestizo culture, the Lenca are gradually losing their identity as a distinct people. The same fate awaits other smaller Amerindian groups in remote mountain areas; these include the Chorti, a Mayan people living along the northwestern border with Guatemala. Only a few hundred Chorti-Maya live on the Honduras side of the border, but about 15,000 live in Guatemala.

Non-Mayan Amerindians such as the Chorotega are also losing their traditions and ethnic identity. The Chorotega in Honduras are descendents of one of the groups that migrated south from Mexico after the Mayan civilization collapsed. Only a few thousand in number, the Chorotega, like other small ethnic groups, find that the economic benefits of assimilating outweigh the benefits of living traditional lifestyles.

Two other small tribal groups are even smaller than the Chorotega. The Pipil and the Hicaque each number fewer than 500 people. Many of these tribal people lived in the fertile valleys of the central and western mountains before Hurricane Mitch displaced them in 1998. Both of these tribes experienced rapid assimilation after they were forced to relocate to larger towns.

Several distinct ethnic groups in Honduras are neither mestizo nor Amerindian. Two share similar cultural backgrounds. The smaller of these two inhabit the Islas de la Bahia, the Bay Islands. Settled by the British, the islands have a different language and religion from the mainland. The small mixed population of the Bay Islands is descended from freed black slaves and Caribbean British settlers who came to Honduras in the nineteenth century. Their unique culture is a combination of colonial British and Afro-Caribbean. Caribbean English creole, rather than Spanish, is the dominant language. Finally, unlike the rest of Honduras, the people are not traditional Roman

Honduras's largest Amerindian group is the Lenca, who largely live in the western and southern highlands. Here, Lenca gather outside a hotel in Tegucigalpa to protest a free-trade agreement between the European Union and the countries of Central America. The agreement would pave the way for international banks to develop parts of the Lenca homeland, which would disrupt their way of life.

Catholics. The Bay Islands are the only portion of the country with an old preevangelical Protestant community.

A much larger group lives along the coast in Belize, Guatemala, and Honduras. These are the people known as Black Caribs, or Garifuna. They are descendents of freed slaves and Amerindians who were forced to migrate early in the nineteenth century from the British Caribbean island of St. Vincent. They live in small coastal villages north and south of the Bay of Honduras. Their culture is an exotic blend of West African, European, and Amerindian elements. Fiercely proud of their heritage, some Black Caribs prefer to be called Garinagu, the Africanized name for Garifuna. They practice unique forms of ancestor worship and animal sacrifice derived from African traditions.

The Garifuna also keep alive African craft designs and create vivid basketry and decorative weavings sought by international art collectors. Their music is also becoming world famous. Melding traditional West African rhythms with Amerindian percussive instrumentation, it initially gained popularity in Honduras as dance music. Known as *punta*, this musical form has roots in traditional Garifuna folk music. Using African rhythms, punta musicians combine electric instruments with traditional turtle shell shakers, rattles, conch shells, and maracas. Now heard by people throughout Central America and the Caribbean, "punta rock" has recently been popularized to some degree in the United States.

The largest non-Hispanic ethnic group in Honduras lives in the region known as Mosquitia, or the Mosquito Coast. The Miskito people live in small communities scattered across the lowlands and savannahs of northeastern Honduras and neighboring Nicaragua. Still relatively unknown to outsiders, Mosquitio is the largest intact wilderness area in Central America. About 10,000 Miskitos live here. This remote area was a haven for escaped slaves. They found refuge with remnants of Amerindian tribes, freed slaves, and a small population of British traders, pirates, and others who sought freedom in the isolated wilderness. The singular culture of the Miskitos was the result of intermarriage among these groups. Until very recently, all Miskitos lived subsistence lifestyles, fishing, hunting, and farming in the isolated lowlands along the Caribbean. Since the Miskitos have not retained strong elements of West African culture like the Black Caribs, most Hondurans consider them to be indigenous people.

CHAPTER

5

Government and Politics

The Honduran government is easy for any student of the U.S. political system to understand, because it shares many of the basic features of the U.S. system. Like the United States, Honduras is a constitutional democratic republic. Although democracy has been denied to the citizens of Honduras for much of its history, today open elections have become routine. Hondurans have quickly embraced the reality of democracy and enjoy regular elections in a festive atmosphere.

The current constitution, written in 1982 and amended many times since, is the sixteenth in the country's history. After decades of political trial and error, corruption, and the suspension of constitutional rights by military juntas, Honduras has settled the question of what form of government works best. Roughly based on the U.S. Constitution, the Honduran framework provides for three branches of government: the executive, legislative, and judicial. Powers among the three are separated, as they are in the United States, to ensure that no one branch can exert total control. Checks and balances is the term for this separation. Although the country has improved its system of separated powers considerably during the past few years, critics complain that the walls of separation between the branches are not as strong as they should be.

BRANCHES OF GOVERNMENT

The most powerful of the three branches, the executive, is headed by a president who is elected to a four-year term. Unlike the United States, which has an electoral college system, the Honduran president is elected directly by popular vote. Three additional designates are also elected; these function as vice presidents. The president appoints members of his Council of Ministers, or cabinet. The president and vice presidents must be Honduran citizens by birth and must be at least 30 years old. The current constitution restricts public servants, general officers of the armed forces, and senior officers of the police from running for the office of president. After years of abuse at the hands of military leaders who seized power in coups, Hondurans are somewhat suspicious of the military. As a result, they have taken constitutional steps to curb the political role of the military.

The legislative branch is unicameral (it has one house). Members of Congress are also elected to four-year terms. Until the 2005 elections, congressional seats were assigned in proportion to the number of votes each party received in an election. The judicial branch is comprised of a Supreme Court of Justice, which, like the U.S. Supreme Court, rules on matters having to do with the constitution. Other levels of the judicial branch are also similar to that of the United States. An appeals court system hears cases from lower courts, and special courts have jurisdiction over criminal, tax, and labor cases. Supreme Court judges are appointed by Congress and confirmed by the president. Strengthening the political independence of the Honduran courts has been a priority for several recent presidents. Much progress has been made, but some observers charge that judges in the high court system are still subject to political influence and corruption.

ADMINISTRATIVE DIVISIONS

The country is divided into 18 administrative subdivisions or regional governments called departments, roughly equivalent to states in the United States. Departments are headed by presidential appointees, called governors, and each department has a designated capital city. Governors represent the formal link between the executive branch and the regional governments and hold considerable power. Departments are further divided into 291 subregional local governments, *municipios*, including a Central District, consisting of the cities of Tegucigalpa and Comayagüela, jointly the national capital. As a department is roughly similar to a U.S. state, a municipio is similar in jurisdiction to a U.S. county. Just as in the county system, municipios may contain more than one city, as well as *aldeas* (villages) and *caseríos* (hamlets). Cities may be divided into smaller administrative divisions known as *colonias* (colonies) and barrios (neighborhoods). The chief executive of the municipio is the mayor, or *alcalde*.

HONDURAN POLITICS

Like the United States, national politics is dominated by two major parties. The Liberal Party is a descendent of the nineteenth-century party that challenged Honduras's entrenched postcolonial establishment. Today, the Liberals represent labor interests but also advocate free trade and foreign investment. The National Party is more conservative and reflects the ongoing concerns that many Hondurans have about rapid change and foreign interference. Other recognized parties that attract some support from voters include the Innovation and National Unity Party, the Christian Democratic Party, and the Democratic Unification Party.

In addition to formal political parties, special interest groups play an increasingly active and legitimate role in Honduran politics, as they do in the United States. From the era of banana company domination in the early twentieth century, the labor movement has been one of the strongest in Central America. By the mid-1990s, trade unions represented almost 20 percent of the Honduran workforce and enjoyed considerable political influence. An organized movement of landless peasants helped bring about some agricultural reform in the early 1960s and 1970s. Today, peasant groups have a small but well-respected voice in national political debate. Beginning in the 1990s, several ethnic-based organizations gained national attention by representing Hondurans of African origin, as well as the country's Amerindian population. Today, these and a number of other interest groups contribute to political discourse in Honduras. Among such groups are those representing women's interests, human rights, and environmental concerns.

POLITICAL TURBULENCE

Honduras achieved independence in 1821 together with Spain's other Central American colonies. Under direct colonial rule, Honduras was administered in a haphazard manner by people who were looking for quick riches. After an initial boom in gold mining peaked in the sixteenth century, Honduras was considered a backwater by the wealthier colonies. Honduras was a founding member of the first of several attempts at a union of Central American states in 1823. The federation collapsed in 1838, and for the decades that followed, Honduran politics was a battleground between conservatives and liberals. At the turn of the twentieth century, U.S.-based banana companies, in particular the United Fruit Company, dominated the government. Politicians defined themselves in terms of their relationship to the foreign companies and the vast foreign-owned plantations that became the center of the Honduran economy until after World War II.

After the turmoil of the Great Depression and World War II, Honduran politics took a turn to the far right. The authoritarian Tiburcio Carias Andino controlled the country until 1948; his rule was followed by two other far-right administrations.

In 1955, a military coup established a provisional government and made open assembly elections possible in 1957. The newly elected assembly appointed Ramón Villeda Morales president. His Liberal Party ruled the country until 1963. In that year, another military coup ousted Villeda, and the military governed Honduras until 1970. After the infamous "Soccer War" of 1969, public discontent over the military's misconduct during the conflict led to the rise of a civilian president, Ramón Cruz of the National Party. Cruz was unable to consolidate his power and, in 1972, another coup toppled him. He was replaced by yet another military ruler, General Lopez, who adopted progressive land reform policies before corruption scandals brought an end to his presidency in 1975. Two more generals led Honduras into the early 1980s.

As we saw in Chapter 3, Honduras was heavily involved in the politics of Guatemala, El Salvador, and Nicaragua during the 1970s and 1980s. The United States viewed Honduras as the Central American country most stable and friendly to its interests. In neighboring Nicaragua, dictator Anastasio Somoza was overthrown in 1979, and civil wars in El Salvador and Guatemala were growing in brutality. Borders between countries were routinely crossed by insurgents, national security forces, and refugees fleeing the violence.

A NEW ERA OF POLITICAL STABILITY

In the midst of this regional chaos, Hondurans held elections in 1981, adopted a new constitution the following year, and put a Liberal Party president, Roberto Suazo Cordoba, in office. As the only peaceful country of its size in Central America, Honduras became the recipient of massive U.S. aid. Economic development projects sponsored by the U.S. Agency for International Development (USAID) brought hundreds of millions of dollars to the country. The world's largest U.S. Peace Corps mission was established in the 1980s.

After a close election in 1985, the first peaceful transfer of power in more than 30 years took place as Rafael Leonardo

Callejas took office in 1986. Callejas was reelected in 1990. Scandals involving government corruption and political influence peddling led to the election of a Liberal Party candidate in 1993, Carlos Roberto Reina.

President Reina successfully prosecuted corrupt government officials as well as some former government and military leaders responsible for human rights abuses in the 1980s. Not only did Reina bring fiscal responsibility to the government, but he also increased civilian control over the military. He is credited with being the first national leader to call for military accountability.

Only a few months after taking office in 1998, the next Honduran president, the Liberal Party's Carlos Roberto Flores Facussé, faced an unprecedented disaster. In October, Hurricane Mitch struck Honduras, killing thousands of people and displacing nearly 2 million others. Estimates of the economic loss were more than $3 billion, nearly one-third of the Honduran GDP at the time! The national transportation infrastructure and the agricultural sector were especially hard hit. In the years after Mitch, Flores and his reformist government managed more than $600 million in disaster and redevelopment assistance from international donors. Despite Flores's success, the damage Mitch inflicted was so great that the country is only now fully recovering. Throughout the rebuilding efforts, Flores made good on his election promise of bringing a moral revolution to Honduras. He created an anticorruption commission, reformed the penal system, and established a civilian Minister of Defense.

A National Party candidate, Ricardo Maduro Joest, won the 2001 presidential election and was inaugurated in 2002. Maduro led Honduras in a national effort to reduce the country's crime and gang problem. He was also a strong supporter of the U.S.-led coalition war in Iraq, even deploying a small contingent of Honduran troops to the Middle East for a short time. Perhaps of more importance, Maduro negotiated and ratified the U.S.-Central America Free Trade Agreement (CAFTA). This bold move led to a reduction in Honduras's international debt,

In late October and early November 1998, Hurricane Mitch devastated Honduras. The Category 5 storm brought more than 30 inches of rain to some parts of the country and caused $900 million worth of damage. Here, abandoned cars are engulfed by floodwaters in the Barrio La Hoya District of Tegucigalpa during the hurricane.

making the country eligible for development grants and programs from the United States and international lenders. Honduras also became the first Central American country to sign a Millennium Challenge Account compact with the United States.

In the 2005 elections, José Manuel "Mel" Zelaya Rosales of the Liberal Party won the presidency by a close 4 percent margin. During the campaign, Zelaya promised to increase transparency in government budgeting and to renew the government's efforts to fight narcotrafficking. Although Honduras is not a major producer of drugs, it is a major transshipment point for cocaine headed for the U.S. market from Panama, Colombia, and other places. Zelaya's theme on the campaign trail was "citizen power." He vowed to continue the economic initiatives of the Maduro government to boost the economy and raise the standard of living. The 2005 elections marked an important change in how legislative seats are filled. For the first time, Hondurans were asked to vote for individual members of Congress rather than for party lists.

By 2007, Zelaya's leadership began to face mounting criticism from conservatives, including the U.S. government. Several events contributed to the growing political storm. In October 2007, Zelaya visited Cuba, becoming the first Honduran president to make an official trip to the communist-controlled island country in nearly a half-century. Less than a year later, he further antagonized not only conservatives within his own country, but the U.S. government as well. The fallout was triggered by Zelaya's committing Honduras to membership in the Bolivarian Alternative for the Americas (ALBA). The group, dominated by strongly leftist Latin American leaders, is headed by Hugo Chavez, Venezuela's liberal populist president and an outspoken critic of U.S. policies. ALBA is opposed to U.S. backed free trade (such as the largely U.S. brokered Central American Free Trade Agreement, or CAFTA).

In June, 2009, acting on orders of the Honduran Supreme Court, the military forcibly removed President Zelaya from office. The court feared that Zelaya was attempting to change the constitution and remove limits to the number of terms a president could serve. It also feared that he was attempting to impose socialism on the country. Speaker of Congress Roberto Micheletti became acting president until an election could be held. In November, Porfirio "Pepe" Lobo Sosa, candidate of the conservative National Party, was elected president. He turned back both the candidate of Zelaya's Liberal Party and interim president Roberto Micheletti. Porfirio Lobo was sworn in as president in January, 2010. Ousted former president Manuel Zelaya went into exile in the Dominican Republic.

The Honduran Constitution guarantees freedom of speech and of the press, and generally, these rights are respected. Nevertheless, some international observers have charged the Honduran media with corruption and political bias. U.S. media and human rights organizations have also identified self-censorship and corruption as ongoing problems. Bribing journalists in return for politically favorable spins on the news is an important issue, although not one unique to Honduras. In the mid-1990s, one media watch group estimated that almost half of the journalists in the country accepted payoffs from political parties, government institutions, businesses, or the military. Despite these serious credibility problems, the Honduran media has played an important role in opening Honduran society to political debate and to criticism of government leaders and policies. Honduras has five daily national newspapers that, like some in the United States, have well-known party affiliations and regularly endorse candidates for election. The idea of a free and objective press that safeguards the public's freedom is a work in progress for Hondurans.

RELATIONS WITH THE UNITED STATES

Since gaining independence from Spain, Honduras has been influenced more by the United States than by any other country. This doesn't necessarily mean that the United States has led Honduran politicians in creating specific policies. In terms of general ideological and economic direction, though, no one doubts that the United States helped shape the country's internal development and that today it continues to bear considerable influence on Honduras's leadership. Direct U.S. involvement dates to the entry of American-owned banana companies into Honduras. Protecting banana company interests became a routine activity for the U.S. military. At various times in the twentieth century, naval vessels, Marine contingents, and army forces were sent in to the country to quell uprisings and protect plantation properties, port facilities, and railroads.

After World War II, relations between the countries changed. The United States wanted to continue its military presence in Central America on a formal basis and signed several agreements with Honduras. One gave the United States a naval base at Trujillo, on the Caribbean coast. Another made it possible for U.S. forces to conduct training exercises in the tropical forests of the country. In return, Honduras received rural development and food assistance and also military aid. The geopolitical significance of the country became apparent in the 1980s, when regional politics exploded. The Contras used Honduran territory as a base from which to invade Nicaragua and fight the Sandinista government. Refugees fleeing the civil wars in Guatemala and El Salvador routinely crossed the Honduran border searching for a safe place to live.

From the perspective of 1980s international relations, there was no end in sight to the cold war between the United States and the Soviet Union. The United States viewed the rise of socialist Nicaraguan Sandinistas as a hemispheric threat. The civil wars in El Salvador and Guatemala were also seen as pieces of the same global game masterminded by the Soviet Union. Honduras sat at the crossroads of this regional conflict, and the United States regarded the country as the geopolitical lynchpin of Central America. Military agreements between the two countries were signed, giving the United States an air base outside the capital city of Tegucigalpa. The U.S. military stationed there supported the Honduran efforts at border protection and also worked on road building and health projects. In addition, the base was used to provide support for El Salvador in its war with leftist revolutionaries.

At the same time that military ties were being strengthened, economic cooperation became a political goal for Honduran leaders. In 1984, the Caribbean Basin Initiative established duty-free access to the U.S. market for Central American goods. The Honduran economy began to grow as a direct result, although other countries in the region, such as Costa Rica, benefited far more. As part of its cold war strategy to win friends for democracy, the United States provided Honduras with massive amounts of assistance in the form of economic development, food donations, health-care aid, and, of course, continuing military aid. In the turbulent decade of the 1980s, U.S. aid to Honduras amounted to more than $1.6 billion.

In the 1990s, U.S. relations with Honduras changed yet again, as the regional wars slowly came to an end. Critics of foreign aid, both in Honduras and the United States, pointed out that Honduran leaders had become dependent on U.S. assistance. They had not undertaken any economic reforms that would address the issue of ongoing poverty. The country was still one of the poorest in the Western Hemisphere. U.S. aid money poured in year after year, yet nothing really changed. According to a former United States ambassador to Honduras, "If there was a significant flaw in our assistance, it was that we did not sufficiently condition aid to macroeconomic reforms and the strengthening of democratic institutions such as the administration of justice." Honduran politicians became serious about reform when they realized that U.S. aid would not always be forthcoming.

Other critics of U.S.-Honduran relations charged that the United States was more interested in using Honduras as a base to fight the Contra War and the war in El Salvador than in helping the country develop. Human rights abuses were tolerated by the United States because the Honduran government was cooperating militarily. Other critics charged that, in the early 1980s, the U.S. embassy in Tegucigalpa was a front for the Contra War rather than a functioning embassy focused on Honduran issues. By the early 1990s, annual U.S. aid began to fall dramatically, from $213 million in 1990 to $60 million in 1993. Military assistance also slowed substantially once the Cold War was over. In 1993, the United States spent only $2.6 million on military aid to Honduras. Although official aid was falling, the United States provided another type of support that in the long run is probably more significant to the country's well-being. As a reward for Honduras's reliability as a Central American ally, the United States forgave $434 million in official debt, almost 96 percent of Honduras's total debt to the United States and about 12 percent of Honduras's total external debt.

During the early 1980s, when the U.S. government aided Nicaraguan counterrevolutionaries known as the Contras in their armed conflict with the leftist Sandinistas, the U.S. military often used Honduras as its base of operations. Here, a special operations soldier instructs Contra fighters at a secret base in Honduras in June 1983.

THE TWENTY-FIRST CENTURY

Despite the end of various regional conflicts by the early 1990s, the United States still maintains a low-profile military outpost at the Enrique Soto Cano Air Base. Soldiers stationed there conduct training exercises for thousands of U.S. National Guardsmen each year, specializing in road-building exercises and in providing basic medical assistance to isolated rural areas. Increasingly, the U.S. military in Honduras is involved in tracking and intercepting drug flights from South America. Honduras is a vital link in the Caribbean-wide radar network maintained by the United States in its war on drugs. U.S. homeland security is another new priority for military forces in Central America.

At the turn of the century, the United States remained Honduras's most important trading partner. After years of political negotiation between Honduras (and its neighbors) and the United States, the Central American Free Trade Agreement (CAFTA) was signed in May 2004. With the addition of the Dominican Republic a few months later, the historic agreement became known as CAFTA-DR. In Honduras, the agreement went into effect on April 1, 2006. CAFTA removes trade and investment barriers and strengthens economic integration in the region. Honduras and the other countries who signed agreed to a number of reforms to enhance and speed up market liberalization.

Among CAFTA's many goals are increased transparency (accountability) in government budgets and procurement and the protection of intellectual property rights. Because the United States is the most important source of foreign investment in Honduras, this last item was of particular importance for the United States. In the 1990s, the issue of violation of intellectual property rights was a point of controversy between the two countries and a sticking point in the CAFTA negotiations. In 1992, the Motion Picture Exporters Association of America and the Office of the United States Trade Representative (USTR) lodged a formal complaint against Honduras, alleging that Honduran cable companies pirated U.S. satellite signals. An investigation was launched and the allegations were found to be accurate. The United States demanded that the Honduran government take steps to protect private satellite television signals. In response, the Honduran government passed comprehensive intellectual property rights legislation in 1993.

Now that most of the political aspects of CAFTA have been settled and the agreement is being implemented, the economic future of Honduras is brighter than at any time in recent history. In Chapter 6, we will examine some of the details of CAFTA, survey the rapid industrialization of the country with help from foreign investors, and look at the traditional mainstays of the national economy.

6

Honduras's Economy

D espite improvements in living standards during the last decade, Honduras remains one of the poorest countries in the Western Hemisphere. The World Bank classifies it as a lower middle-income country. Although growth of the national economy during recent years averaged around 5 percent, growth slowed toward the end of the decade. By 2009, it actually declined by an estimated 3 percent. Although the unemployment rate in 2010 was estimated to be around 3 percent (one of the lowest in the world), six of every 10 Hondurans continue to live in poverty. A sure sign of economic weakness is in rates of remittance. Remittances from Honduran wage earners living abroad, mainly in the United States, represent about 15 percent of the country's foreign exchange, more than $2 billion in 2006, averaging about 2.5 billion annually during recent years.

Recent governments have attempted to move the economy beyond a dependence on agricultural and natural resource exports, and progress is being made in some areas. Old problems persist and new issues challenge the government, however. Today, the government has made poverty reduction its top priority. The government has identified several goals to stimulate the economy: generating jobs, good governance through state modernization and civic participation, environmental protection and risk management, and development of human capital.

The Central American Free Trade Agreement (CAFTA-DR) offers Honduras the best chance to find a way out of the persistent poverty that has plagued the country since independence. The agreement also includes El Salvador, Guatemala, Nicaragua, and Costa Rica, plus the United States and the Dominican Republic. Modeled on the North American Free Trade Agreement (NAFTA), CAFTA is an attempt at full economic integration among the member states. Honduras was part of the U.S.-Caribbean Basin Initiative in the 1970s, which gave preferential treatment to certain Honduran exports. In contrast, CAFTA is a comprehensive agreement under which virtually all Honduran goods and services will be included eventually in a marketplace of almost 350 million people.

CAFTA may be viewed in the light of earlier efforts at union that Honduras has made. In Chapter 3, we reviewed the attempts that Central American countries had made to create a political federation. Although these attempts failed, they reveal a belief in mutual cooperation that has led to CAFTA. The United States was not part of those early attempts. With guidance from the United States, CAFTA represents the biggest, and some might say, riskiest, effort yet.

Before we look at some of the details of CAFTA, it is important to identify problems that Honduras faces in its quest for economic growth. One overarching issue with which the government must come to grips is the stiff competition Honduras faces from its neighbors for foreign direct investment (FDI). Although we have seen many similarities in climate, landscape, and culture between Honduras and its Central American neighbors, several important differences between Honduras and its neighbors have proved to be disadvantages to Honduras in attracting FDI. Far surpassing official aid that states of the world receive, FDI makes a crucial difference between places that grow and others that stagnate.

One drawback facing Honduras is its transportation and energy infrastructure. Built for the most part by the banana and coffee industries from 1920 to the 1960s, the transportation network is old and outdated and does not meet the country's present needs. Another drawback to international investors is the quality of the workforce. Like its neighbors, Honduras has many unemployed workers eager for jobs, and managers of most foreign-owned firms report that Hondurans are easily trained and are eager workers. Labor unions have a long history in the country, though, dating to the earliest years of the banana era. Strikes among some labor sectors are common, and even national strikes have been threatened as recently as 10 years ago.

One problem hampering economic growth is the steady migration of people from the countryside to the cities. As rural agriculture declines as a way to make a living, workers move to the city, searching for jobs. High urban unemployment results, together with sprawling suburban slums and chronic crime. Foreign companies seeking to relocate assembly plants or to otherwise invest in Central America often choose one of Honduras's neighbors, such as Costa Rica. These and other political and social issues impede Honduran development, but if CAFTA is implemented properly, real change may happen soon.

GOING GLOBAL

Under CAFTA-DR, almost 80 percent of U.S. consumer goods now enter Honduras without being charged any customs duty. All tariffs not already lifted will be phased out during a period of time, nearly all by 2015. Textile and apparel goods are traded between the two countries without any duties or quotas, in

In May 2004, representatives from the Central American countries of Costa Rica, El Salvador, Guatemala, Honduras, and Nicaragua signed the Central American Free Trade Agreement (CAFTA) with the United States. Pictured here, from left to right: Alberto Trejos of Costa Rica, Miguel Lacayo of El Salvador, Robert B. Zoellick of the United States, Marcio Cuevas of Guatemala, Norman Garcia of Honduras, and Mario Arana of Nicaragua.

most cases. Some U.S. textile and clothing manufacturers have been hurt by the loss of business. Other U.S. companies, however, specializing in fabric, yarn, or fiber production have seen their businesses grow under the agreement.

CAFTA also has increased agricultural trade dramatically. About half of U.S. agricultural exports to Honduras are now duty-free, expanding the market for many U.S. food products. The reduction of tariffs and liberalization of trade generally attracts investors in newer export industries such as cigar manufacturing, insurance, and brewing. Now that CAFTA is being implemented, Honduran energy generation and telecommunications are also beginning to attract investors.

Government customs policies are a target area for reform under the agreement. Honduras and the other Central American states agree to make customs processes fair and open to public scrutiny. They also agree to crack down on illegal international shipment of products. Regulations for ensuring sanitary food products are being strictly enforced. As a result, trade in pork, poultry, and dairy products will be likely to increase substantially.

For years, one problem in the otherwise good relations between the United States and Honduras has been the widespread violation of U.S. copyright law. In 2006, the Honduran Congress passed legislation strengthening protection of intellectual property rights (IPR), in order for the country to meet full compliance with CAFTA-DR. The CAFTA regulations are consistent with U.S. standards of protection and enforcement. The new Honduran laws now fully protect a wide range of intellectual property, including computer software, music, books, videos, and U.S. patents and trademarks. Penalties for pirating and counterfeiting have been stiffened. Shortly after the Congress passed the new regulations, government agents launched a series of highly publicized raids on producers and sellers of pirated U.S. software, CDs, and DVDs.

Because protection of intellectual property is critical in creating partnership opportunities between the United States and other CAFTA countries, the new Honduran laws and enforcement efforts are a welcome change. One U.S. company testing the new waters of IPR is the NFL's New Orleans Saints. The Saints embarked on a trade mission in 2006 to explore the possible expansion of professional football into the Honduran market. The team's negotiators signed an agreement with the largest sports club in Honduras, Olimpia Deportivo. The result is a partnership that allows the Saints to sell their trademark sports memorabilia exclusively through Olimpia.

Themed sports merchandise has long been a lucrative target for counterfeiters in Central America and elsewhere. Team owners feel comfortable enough with the new regulations, however, to allow licensing of the Saints logo in Honduras. Marketing visits by Saints players and regular training exchanges are also part of the arrangement. In a separate negotiation, the Saints have finalized a partnership with Corporación Televicentro to broadcast their games in Spanish on Honduran television. Before the passage of CAFTA and the new Honduran laws, encrypted satellite signals were commonly intercepted by unscrupulous providers in Honduras. They, in turn, redistributed U.S. television programming illegally.

DEVELOPING THE PRIMARY ECONOMY

Although CAFTA sets into place the framework needed for future growth, many of Honduras's traditional economic activities remain relatively unchanged. In the primary economic sector, change and continuity may both be found. The primary sector includes those industries that directly exploit natural resources, such as agriculture, mining, timber, and fishing.

Since colonial times, the Honduran economy has been almost totally dependent on the primary sector. During the nineteenth century, the extraction and exporting of minerals— particularly gold, silver, and zinc—provided most foreign revenue. The most productive mines were owned by a company headquartered in the United States, the New York and Honduras Rosario Mining Company. Silver accounted for about 55 percent of exports in the 1880s. Mining stimulated the growth of some ancillary businesses and resulted in the construction of some roads and railroads, but long-term economic benefits were generally few. Mining was never well integrated into the rest of the Honduran economy. It employed few workers and provided little government revenue.

With the emergence of the banana industry in the early years of the twentieth century, however, the Honduran export economy boomed. Agricultural exports to the United States went from $3 million in 1913 to more than $25 million by

1929. The Honduran economy's dependence on bananas continued until after midcentury. The banana labor force during these years represented a large share of Honduran wage earners. In 1954, more than 35,000 Hondurans worked for the United Fruit Company or the Standard Fruit Company.

During the 1950s, the Honduran government, encouraged by high international export prices, worked to diversify its agricultural sector. Beef, cotton, sugar, and especially coffee became important exports. By 1960, bananas had declined to about 45 percent of total export earnings.

By the 1970s, coffee exports surpassed bananas as Honduras's leading agricultural export. A coffee crisis brought on by global overproduction during the 1980s, however, slowed the growth of the coffee industry considerably. In the 1990s, the banana industry was again booming, as world demand increased and new markets opened up.

Like other underdeveloped countries dependent on agriculture exports, the Honduran economy suffers from market fluctuations and is vulnerable to external shocks. World competition in banana and coffee production and marketing has resulted in the loss of about one-third of the Honduran agricultural sector's purchasing power since the 1980s. Sometimes competition from other primary-sector-exporting countries combines with natural disasters to pack a one-two punch to national economies.

In 1998, Hurricane Mitch devastated banana and coffee crops. Small farmers, who account for nearly 90 percent of coffee producers and almost half of Honduras's production, were hit hardest. By 2001, coffee earnings had fallen by about 35 percent. Overall, nearly 40 percent of GDP was lost in the 1998 hurricane season. Coffee producers were already suffering, however: Newer producers, such as Vietnam, were taking larger shares of the world market. In addition, Honduras has never been successful in branding its coffee, unlike its neighbors. Both Guatemala and Costa Rica have managed to make their names synonymous with high-quality specialty coffees.

Bananas and coffee account for the majority of Honduras's export revenues, but these industries have yet to recover from the devastation inflicted by Hurricane Mitch in 1998. Here, a boy picks coffee beans on a farm in eastern Honduras, four years after the hurricane.

Honduran coffee shares many of the same qualities as beans grown nearby, but it has never been marketed as well.

Expanding agricultural production as a solution to competition and natural hazards would be difficult in Honduras. In coffee production, much of the suitable land has already been brought under cultivation. Mountain and hill soils in Honduras lack the thick volcanic ash that makes coffee growing more lucrative in Guatemala and Costa Rica. Historically, Honduran coffee production has been characterized by low yields compared to its Central American competitors. Coffee yields in Costa Rica, for instance, are almost twice those of Honduras.

Reasons for this situation are complex. In the past, rather than using improved techniques, farmers have expanded the land under cultivation in order to increase productivity. This means that farms have been pushed farther into forested lands and areas with marginally productive soils. Deforestation and erosion have been the long-term results. Legal problems with land titles have also contributed to the problems faced by Honduras's many small farmers. Without undisputed title to land, farmers have been unable to get credit for improvements, fertilizers, or equipment. After years of agitation by peasants' groups and farmers, in the 1990s, the Honduran Congress enacted the Agricultural Modernization Law. The legal process for issuing land titles was simplified, and the land cooperatives formed in the 1960s were allowed to individualize their holdings so that they might be sold.

Throughout the 1990s, small banana producers went out of business as they sold their newly titled land to multinational banana companies. After years of wrangling over access to the European Union's (EU's) lucrative banana market, the big companies that dominated banana production for most of the twentieth century won an increase in Honduras's banana quota to the EU. This was one round in the ongoing banana war between the EU and the United States. Europe's demand for bananas is only slightly behind North America's. The EU protects banana producers in former British and French colonies. It does this by placing high import tariffs on fruit from noncolonial regions. The upshot is that the United States and the EU are engaged in a long-range series of negotiations over banana quotas, tariffs, customs, and market access. As a result of the slight opening in the European market for noncolonial bananas, the big U.S. companies saw an increase in demand, market share, and profits. Again, as in the early years of the banana boom, the big companies were hungry for new land to bring under cultivation. This time the growth in demand was from the EU. Two U.S.-based multinationals, Chiquita Brands International and Dole Food Company, now directly produce almost all Honduran bananas. Chiquita bought out United Fruit Company, and Dole purchased Standard Fruit Company. So, in a sense the domination of Honduran exports by the foreign firms has continued for a century. The names may be different, but the practices are almost identical as those of the early twentieth century.

One significant change has occurred in the banana business. Until the 1980s, the U.S. companies controlled the production quota, management practices, exporting, and marketing. Much of the actual crop production, however, was still in the hands of small independent banana producers banded together in cooperatives. Some of these farmers still sold their crops to the big companies as late as the 1980s. By the 1990s, though, these small producers were disappearing. Economic stagnation made land sales to the big companies attractive, and the Agricultural Modernization Law made land titling and sales easy.

The so-called banana war between U.S.-based companies and the EU is not yet over, but for now, the Honduran banana industry is relatively stable. The same cannot be said of the coffee industry. Although Honduran banana production is dominated by multinational giants, such is not the case with coffee. This commercial crop is grown by more than 50,000 small producers. As prices continue to fluctuate, many of these smaller farmers are forced out of the coffee-growing business and their lands are converted to other uses.

In the 1980s and 1990s, Honduras began developing some of its other natural resources. Agricultural crops such as melons and pineapples became important export items, as did animal feed. The shrimp and lobster industry grew quickly, as world demand for seafood rose sharply each year. Despite the serious setbacks caused by coastal flooding associated with Hurricane Mitch, Honduran shrimp and lobster exports have grown steadily. Farmed shrimp now dominate exports. In its first years, Honduran producers depended on laboratory shrimp larvae from the United States. Conflicts developed between independent shrimpers who still set out into coastal waters to catch wild shrimp and the corporate-backed producers who use aquaculture technology. Shrimpers charged that corporate methods damaged the environment and destroyed the mangrove swamps that are natural breeding areas for wild shrimp. Corporate aquaculturalists began moving inland to take advantage of cheaper lands. A few traditional shrimp-boat fishermen continue to harvest the remaining wild shrimp. Unfortunately, the shrimp industry has not recovered from Mitch's destruction of the country's mangrove swamps.

Forestry has played a modest part in the local Honduran economy for decades. Recently, furniture and other wood products have occupied a small but growing place in the national export economy. As in other Central American countries, however, Honduras's forest cover has been slowly vanishing. Commercial exploitation is part of the problem. Unregulated logging has taken its toll, but clearing of forest land for cattle ranches is also responsible for much of the loss. During the last half century, Honduras has lost much of its natural forest cover. Some subsistence farmers still clear plots of forest land in order to grow crops for several years, only to move on to another cleared plot when the soils are depleted. Logging of tropical hardwoods, much of it illegal, also contributes to forest loss. The black market in rare timber species is growing as world demand for exotic wood increases.

Until recently, the country has neglected and badly mismanaged its timber resources. Major reforestation legislation was passed in 1992 to promote replanting of cutover forests. The government understands the value of its remaining undeveloped forests to the growing tourist industry, so further protective legislation is expected. Tourism is growing. Honduras shares all the physical features that have made Costa Rica and

Belize popular destinations for eco- and adventure tourism. Additional steps must be taken to protect Honduras's fragile environments, though, before tourism rivals that of its neighbors. Currently the Bay Islands and several of the national parks located in the mountains attract international visitors.

MAQUILAS

Development of the manufacturing and service industries has been slow. The lack of a robust domestic market is one problem. In 2005, manufacturing comprised about 18 percent of gross domestic product (GDP). So far, though, textile manufacturing, agricultural processing, and assembly operations make up the bulk of this sector. The service sector comprises about 53 percent of the GDP. This figure is not as impressive as it might be. Many underemployed people and individuals working in the informal sector are counted as service workers. Foreign direct investment (FDI), which will likely increase under CAFTA-DR, has not matched that made in other Central American countries. More industrially advanced countries in the region compete directly for FDI. For years, Costa Rica has been a leader in attracting international investment. Currently, the United States, then South Korea, Taiwan, and Canada are the biggest foreign investors in Honduras's industrial growth.

U.S. direct investment in Honduras in 2006 increased to $517 million, almost all of it in the *maquila* sector. Maquilas are production facilities primarily for export items. In Honduras, textile and apparel factories create thousands of relatively good-paying jobs. Some drawbacks exist in an export economy, however. The use of local inputs remains minimal in Honduran maquilas. That is, most of the material used in the factories comes from outside the country. Another problem is that the small domestic market means that the goods produced in the country typically are not sold in Honduras, but are exported. Finally, most of the production jobs are low paying.

Maquilas are Honduran production facilities, where export items such as clothing are manufactured. One such maquila is the Southeast Textiles clothing factory in Chaloma, which produces clothing for several hip-hop lines. Above, employees leave the factory after work.

U.S. companies invest in production plants in less-developed countries in order to take advantage of low wages, thereby increasing their profit margin. During CAFTA negotiations, representatives of North Carolina's textile manufacturers opposed lifting the import duties on Central American textiles. They realized that U.S. wages would be severely undercut. Their protests did nothing to slow down the elimination of textile tariffs. Two other selling points for companies investing in maquilas are that labor laws and environmental regulations in Honduras are much less stringent than they are in the United States. In addition, taxes are much lower. More than 130,000 Hondurans now work in the maquilas, many of them earning a dollar an hour or less.

The United States is the country's biggest trading partner, and the maquilas are the basis for much of this trade. Maquila factories import raw textiles and other materials from the United States and produce finished goods for the U.S. market. Well-known U.S. clothing brands such as Levi's, Hanes, and Victoria's Secret all have factories in Honduras, and many lesser-known U.S. firms produce clothing there for chain department stores. The Kentucky–based M. Fine & Sons is one example. The firm produces flannel shirts and jeans for J.C. Penney, K-Mart, and Kohl's stores in two big Honduran factories.

Under Honduras's Temporary Import Law, exporters are allowed to bring raw materials and parts into Honduras with no surcharge or customs duties, as long as the input is used to produce exports. Under this arrangement, up to 5 percent of the export items may be sold locally. Production plants in the special export processing zones pay no import duties on goods or capital equipment. In addition, the production and sale of goods within the export zones enjoy a 10-year exemption from state and municipal income taxes. Companies operating in the zones are permitted to send home all profits and capital. Assembly plants also have access to on-site customs inspectors, making export back to the United States or the world market quick and inexpensive.

The first and biggest free-trade zone (FTZ) in Honduras was built in Puerto Cortés. In 1998, the government extended FTZ benefits to the entire country, and other areas grew quickly. Privately owned industrial parks were granted equal status with official free-trade zones. These areas are operated much as industrial parks are operated in the United States. Today, 27 industrial parks currently operate in Honduras, with more than 80 percent of them in the North Coast region. All are located within a few hours drive of Honduras's major Caribbean ports and San Pedro Sula, a major transportation hub.

Although the government would like to diversify into other types of industry, more than 90 percent of the assembly plants are engaged in the assembly of clothing. One of the great hopes associated with CAFTA is that higher-paying jobs will come to both the industrial parks and to the growing cities in the interior.

7

Regions
of Honduras

D
espite the basic similarities of mestizo culture that hold the people of the country together, ways of life in Honduras vary. Major differences exist in economy, development, topography, and climate. The bustling industrial parks of the North Coast and low-key Bay Islands are worlds apart culturally. So, too, are the bright lights of the big capital city, Tegucigalpa, and the remote and sparsely settled and isolated Mosquito Coast. Significant differences exist between urban and rural dwellers, too. Residents of the biggest cities are much like citizens of big Northern American urban centers. They have access to U.S. popular culture and have an appetite for fast food and the latest fashions. Remote countryside dwellers and subsistence farmers live lifestyles that have remained relatively unchanged for centuries.

NORTH COAST

Honduras's Caribbean coast from Guatemala to Mosquitia is commonly called the North Coast. This region is the country's economic powerhouse. The industrial city of San Pedro Sula is located here, as is the old Caribbean port of La Ceiba and the newer port of Puerto Cortés. Although the western portion of this region is home to most of the country's biggest industrial parks, the central coast depends on tourism. Much of this new industrial development and tourism takes place in the heart of the old banana plantation district. Today, bananas and other fruit such as pineapples and melons are still important mainstays. Standard Fruit Company (now the Dole Food Company), one of the first U.S.-based corporations in Honduras, is still headquartered in La Ceiba. The North Coast region, then, is a microcosm of the Honduran economy, past and present.

La Ceiba, with a population of about 250,000, is the third-largest city in Honduras. Founded in 1877, the city was named for a giant ceiba tree growing near the first dock constructed in the area. La Ceiba quickly became the primary port for banana exports to New Orleans and Mobile. Export agriculture and ecotourism are the basis for the city's economy today.

To the west of La Ceiba is the department of Cortés, which is the country's second-most populous. More than 1.3 million people live here, in the city of San Pedro Sula and numerous agricultural towns in the richly fertile Sula River Valley. Famous for its pristine beaches, Cortés has long attracted tourists, both domestic and international. Much of the country's banana exports originate in this department. Honduras's second-largest Caribbean port, Puerto Cortés, serves the agricultural sector of the Sula River Valley and also the industrial exports of San Pedro Sula, the departmental capital.

San Pedro Sula sits in the Sula Valley, about 37 miles (60 kilometers) inland from Puerto Cortés. With a population of nearly one million, it is the second-largest city in the country behind Tegucigalpa. The city is Honduras's industrial capital. It is home to traditional Honduran industries, such as banana companies and cigar makers. Many foreign-owned assembly plants are located here, including the maquilas that have grown up around the city like mushrooms since the early 1990s. The city was founded by Pedro de Alvarado in 1536. It was located near the rich Minas de Sula gold mines and grew quickly as a mining supply center. When gold and silver were discovered farther to the east, many of the settlers left and the town became a quiet backwater. For much of its history, the city was little more than a large agricultural settlement. In the 1920s, however, explosive population growth followed the booming market for bananas. When a rail line linked the inland plantations with Puerto Cortes, the city was poised to become the country's industrial and agricultural center.

San Pedro Sula has a reputation for productivity throughout Central America. A sizable immigrant population has been drawn to the city by its business opportunities. Working in various aspects of the maquila sector, Palestinians and, in particular, East Asians, play important roles in the garment assembly plants. Although Honduras ranks close to the bottom of the World Economic Forum's Growth Competitive Index (seventy-sixth among 80 listed countries), the city of San Pedro Sula is an exception. With a skilled workforce, a modern and efficient international airport, and a commitment to working with foreign investors, the city is far ahead of its Honduran competitors.

Farther to the east along the North Coast, the department of Colón contains the old port of Trujillo, originally a shipment point for gold, and later a minor banana port. Trujillo is a sharp contrast to the high-quality tourism of the western beaches or the glitter of San Pedro Sula. Life here is more akin to the Bay Islands. An appealing Caribbean pace characterizes the lifestyle of many of the people. Low-key tourism and some agriculture are the main businesses. The city boasts that the first Catholic Mass on the mainland of the Western Hemisphere was held on

Textile factories such as this one are found throughout San Pedro Sula, Honduras's second-largest city. The city is the center of the country's apparel industry, which ranks third behind China and Mexico in supplying the United States with clothing. Here, employees sew pants at the clothing factory.

a site in town. Christopher Columbus stopped here in 1502 and worshiped. Established as a fortified town in 1524, it was briefly the capital of the Honduran colony. Because of its vulnerability to attack by pirates and other colonial powers, however, the Spanish all but abandoned the site in the eighteenth century. One of the principal tourist attractions today is the Spanish fort built on the bluffs above the bay.

Located on a promontory above the Bay of Trujillo, the city today has a population of about 30,000. Just a few miles away, Garifuna people live in three coastal fishing villages—Santa Fe, San Antonio, and Guadalupe. Their presence enhances the exotic nature of life in this quiet stretch of the Honduran coast.

BAY ISLANDS

Life in the Islas de la Bahía, the Bay Islands, is slow compared to the bustle of the North Coast. Beautiful beaches and coral reefs draw adventure tourists, scuba divers, and deep-sea fishermen from around the world. The island group is comprised of Roatán, Guanaja, Utila, Barbareta, the Cochinos Cays, and several smaller islets. These were visited by Columbus on his voyage along the Central American coast, but it was not until the eighteenth century that they began to attract settlers.

Population of the islands today is about 43,000. English is widely spoken, a legacy of the British domination of the islands until the 1860s. Roatán is the largest island in size and population and is the most developed. Some rapid changes have occurred as the island's popularity has put pressure on the fragile environment. In the 1960s and 1970s, the island's visitors were primarily Northern Americans who were looking for inexpensive fishing trips or scuba diving excursions. British soldiers stationed across the Bay of Honduras in Belize visited on weekend passes. Rooms or small huts without electricity attracted people who wanted to rough it in a tropical island setting or who lacked the money for more upscale accommodations.

In the 1970s, roads were unpaved tracks through the forests, and automobiles were a rarity. After Central America's regional wars came to an end in the late 1980s and early 1990s, the tourist industry boomed. Roatán quickly began to develop modern tourist resorts that today attract thousands of people. Commercial airlines service the island from La Ceiba, less than an hour's flight away. The island still offers the chance to

Each year, hundreds of thousands of tourists are drawn to the beautiful beaches of Roatán, which is located off the northern coast of Honduras. Here, a lone tourist walks along West Bay Beach, one of the island's most popular destinations for snorkeling.

watch the sun set over the mainland from a secluded beach, but its primitive tropical character has all but disappeared. The government is busy with plans to build more paved roads, and negotiations are under way to bring a large U.S.-style casino to the island.

The other large islands are not yet as developed as Roatán and still retain some of their unspoiled nature. Utila is famous for its coral reefs. Guanaja, a former refuge for British pirates, is the least developed.

MOSQUITO COAST

Pirates, British and otherwise, are also associated with the history of the easternmost extent of Honduras's Caribbean coast. This is the department of Gracias a Dios (Spanish for *Thanks to God*). The second-largest department in area, Gracias a Dios contains only about 78,000 people. Many of them are Miskito Indians, other Amerindian people, and Afro-Europeans descended from slaves and Caribbean buccaneers. Mestizos are a minority along the Mosquito Coast. The southern and eastern edges of the region are rapidly becoming an agricultural settlement frontier. Subsistence farmers and other people from the more densely populated interior of Honduras are moving to the region in search of available land.

Extensive pine savannas, winding lagoons, and dense swamplands are found along the coast and as far as 40 miles (64 kilometers) or more inland. Many of the smaller settlements here are inaccessible except by boat. Interregional communication is infrequent, and, today, as throughout history, the lack of government authority is occasionally a problem. Only a few of the department's larger towns are routinely linked by air service to the rest of the country. In the south, remnants of tropical rain forest are still found, although these forests are under intense developmental pressure.

Paul Theroux's novel *The Mosquito Coast* narrates the adventures of a Northern American family who move to a small, remote village in coastal Honduras. The novel served as the basis of a popular film starring Harrison Ford that vividly depicts the lush isolation of this part of the country.

URBAN HIGHLANDS

East-west trending mountains that extend across the center of Honduras are home to roughly half the national population. From the dawn of the sixteenth century, Spanish settlers preferred the milder temperatures of the tierra templadas to the coastal heat and humidity. The colonial capitals of Tegucigalpa and Comayagua were located in these cooler heights. Before the arrival of Europeans, Mayans inhabiting the western portion of the country also lived in the tierra templada. Population densities here have always been much greater than those of the more remote eastern mountains.

The country's capital city, Tegucigalpa, is located in the southern extent of the central mountains in the department of Francisco Morazán. Although this relatively small department is one of the two most urbanized in Honduras, it also contains rugged mountains, cloud forests, and one of the country's most famous national parks, La Tigre. Francisco Morazán has a population of more than 1.7 million people.

Tegucigalpa (*Tegus* for short) is the country's largest city, with a metro population of more than 1.3 million people. Founded in 1578 near the site of an Amerindian village, the city was a gold and silver mining center in its early days. The name itself means "silver hills" in the Nahuatl language. After independence, the Honduran capital was moved back and forth several times from Tegus to nearby Comayauga. In 1880, Tegucigalpa became the permanent capital. Today, its former rival is considered a sister city, culturally and politically, and many citizens of Comayagua consider themselves to be capital city residents. At an elevation of about 3,250 feet (990 meters), Tegus has one of the mildest climates of any large Central American city. Unfortunately, the mountain basin in which it is located traps air pollution that creates a Southern California–style haze at certain times of the year.

In the 1970s, rural-to-urban migration began to change the population distribution in Honduras. Subsistence farmers gave up on their cleared forest plots and moved to Tegus and other urban areas looking for jobs. Tegus's population boomed in the 1970s and 1980s, as thousands of migrants flocked to the city. The hills around the old city center became covered with sprawling suburban development. Some of it was planned for the small population of middle-class citizens. Most of it,

The summer months are generally the wettest in Honduras, where up to 200 inches (508 centimers) of rain can fall each year. Here, residents of Tegucigalpa move their possesions from their flooded houses after heavy rains indundated the region in June 2007.

however, was haphazardly built for poorer migrants. These *colonias* have pushed out in all directions, making Tegucigalpa an example of Central American urban sprawl at its worst. The government has been struggling to provide city services, police and fire protection, and education to the burgeoning population. Job creation has also long been a priority for the national government. Today, a few maquilas are located in the Amarateca Valley, on the northern outskirts of the city. These assembly plants provide a few thousand much-needed jobs.

Situated in the mountains far from the Caribbean ports, Tegus is unable to compete effectively with San Pedro Sula and the North Coast for maquila investments. Nevertheless, it is the political, if not the economic, capital of Honduras. As such, it is home to the national legislature, various government agencies, the main campus of the National University of Honduras, and many other schools. Much of the city is new.

North American-style shopping malls have been constructed in the last decade or so, giving parts of the city a generic appearance. Megaplaza is the biggest and newest of these malls. U.S.-based fast-food franchises are increasingly popular, enhancing the bland "anywhereness" of some commercial districts. Some examples of colonial architecture, such as the Basilica of the Virgin of Suyapa, have survived the rapid growth of the past few decades. Some of the city's colonial buildings were lost in 1998 in the flooding brought on by Mitch. Neighborhoods, particularly in the northwest part of town, were completely swept away as the path of the storm slowly crossed the highlands around Tegus. Record rainfall in the area flooded the Choluteca River that runs through the city.

Tegus's traditional competitor for title of Honduran capital is the town of Comayagua. Located just a few miles to the east, the department and town of the same name share the same mountain climate that makes Tegus so comfortable. But Comayagua has not seen the intense migration that changed the character of Tegus so drastically. The departmental population is 390,643 people, but only about 70,000 live in the town. Without the influx of people and spared the destructive flooding of 1998, much of the city's colonial architecture and small-town atmosphere remain intact.

Comayagua is now one of Honduras's most important cultural tourism attractions. The city's many historic landmarks, neighborhoods, and architectural gems are protected from urban renewal projects and encroaching development by the Honduran government. The old central plaza in the city center is the historic and cultural heart of Comayagua. The plaza is a focal point for festival gatherings and concerts. Like central plazas throughout Central America, it is also used daily by urban residents seeking a little greenery and open space in the midst of the city. The neoclassical city hall faces the plaza, as does the beautiful Cathedral of Comayagua, constructed in 1711.

PACIFIC COAST

The urban hub of Honduras's Pacific Coast region is the city of Choluteca, located in the southernmost part of the country. The department borders the Gulf of Fonseca to the west and the country of Nicaragua to the east and south. The city of Choluteca is to the south what San Pedro Sula is to the North Coast—a bustling, productive urban area that attracts people and businesses with its efficient transportation network and modern amenities. With a population of more than 100,000, it is the country's fourth-largest city.

The city site was well chosen by the Spanish in 1522. The narrow Pacific lowlands stretch a few miles south to the Gulf of Fonseca. Situated on the banks of the Choluteca River, the city's prosperity comes in part from the river's rich alluvial valley. Today, it is a processing and export point for melons, watermelons, okra, and sweet potatoes. Shrimp, other seafood, and salt also are exported. At slightly higher elevations a short distance inland, some coffee is grown, most of it for the local market. One drawback to life here is the climate. Residents of Choluteca take perverse pride in their year-round heat and stifling humidity. Although close to the coast, the city is not close enough for ocean breezes to moderate the temperatures.

Because it is the regional center of southern Honduras, Choluteca is a major bus terminal and starting point for travel east and west on the Pan-American Highway (PAH). The PAH is an international highway system that begins at the U.S.-Canadian border and extends to Santiago, Chile. This ambitious road project has taken years to construct and even today it is not complete. Near the Panamanian-Colombian border, a segment of the PAH is not yet finished. Within Central America, most of the PAH is a two-lane, poorly maintained road, but it is an important symbol of international cooperation and communication for people in the region.

Honduras, like its neighbors, suffers from a lack of safe modern roads. Choluteca, unlike most other areas of the country, had a fairly good highway system leading into and out of the city before Hurricane Mitch. The 1998 storm passed well to the north of the city as it moved through the country. Nevertheless, Choluteca was hit hard by flooding. As you learned in Chapter 2, most of Mitch's destruction resulted from river flooding as the storm stalled offshore and then moved very slowly through the highlands. The slow movement produced record rainfalls. Rivers throughout Central America, such as the Choluteca, left their banks, sweeping roads and entire villages away. Tremendous mudslides added to the misery. In three days, the city received more than 36 inches (914 millimeters) of rain! Heavy damage was the result, and the roads linking the department with the outside world, including portions of the PAH, were destroyed.

EASTERN MOUNTAINS

The eastern ranges of Honduras's mountains merge with those of Nicaragua. These peaks are not as high as the western mountains, although rugged topography and low population densities give them a primeval character that attracts ecotourists. Dense evergreen forests and remnants of rain forests are found here. Most of this remote land is found in the largest department in Honduras, Olancho, which is slightly larger than El Salvador. Only about 450,000 people live in this vast territory, most of them in scattered villages where farming, cattle ranching, placer gold mining, and timbering make up the local economy. The region's central plains also are home to extensive cattle ranches and farms. The people hold traditional rural values and are fiercely independent. Olancho was the last piece of the national territory to seriously resist inclusion in Honduras when it became independent. In 2006, the country elected a president, Manuel Zelaya, who hails from one of the towns in this region.

Deforestation is a problem, especially in the extreme east, where subsistence farmers and illegal loggers operate far from any government authority. The Honduran Congress has taken steps to protect this area, but enforcement is difficult in this isolated land. One of the first protected areas in the country was established here in 1980. This park, the largest in the country, is the Río Plátano Biosphere Reserve, which encompasses diverse ecosystems. In the northern portion of the reserve, extensive savannas merge into the Mosquito Coast, where Mosquito and Garifuna communities exist in semi-isolation. To the south, forested mountaintops reach elevations of more than 3,000 feet (1,000 meters). This is an area endangered by chaotic, unregulated development. In this part of the reserve, subsistence farmers push farther into the fragile forests each year, and black market loggers target increasingly rare tropical hardwoods for harvest.

Much of the reserve and the rest of the region have the look and feel of a frontier region. Portions have not been systematically mapped or even explored by outsiders. One of the most startling discoveries of recent years took place just a few miles from President Zelaya's hometown. The Cave of the Glowing Skulls, an ancient burial site, was discovered by Peace Corps volunteers and a group of Hondurans in 1994. It takes its name from the human remains found there that have been covered by calcite, a crystalline form of calcium carbonate, dripping from the cave ceiling. The calcite gives a weird, glowing luminescence to the bones, and local legends persist about lost cities of the Maya that lie waiting discovery beneath dense forest growth.

WESTERN MOUNTAINS

Although at least some coffee is grown in every department in Honduras, the western mountains are famous for its production. The region is a traditional coffee area that continues to produces the best beans for export. Although coffee has been grown for many years, it was not until the mid-twentieth century that it became an important export crop in Honduras. As early as 1858, farmers in the central and western mountains

Illegal logging is a contentious issue in Honduras, where more than 200,000 acres of timber are being cut down per year. Some of this wood is being supplied to American companies, who knowingly purchase the illegally harvested timber. Here, Honduran troops come across a recently harvested section of forest near Salama, in central Honduras.

grew coffee beans, but none were exported. Roads, then as now, were bad; areas of coffee cultivation were small and widely scattered over mountainous terrain. By the late nineteenth century, the country was producing 500,000 pounds (226,796 kilograms) annually, almost all of it for local markets. Today, the commercial Honduran coffee industry continues to face the same old problem of inadequate roads and isolated farms.

Honduran coffee cultivation is perhaps the least mechanized farming in Central America, a region that does not have high levels of industrialized agriculture. Coffee planting and harvesting are labor-intensive activities that employ thousands of people seasonally. Coffee farming is practiced here much as it has been for the last century. In other aspects, Copán and its capital city of Santa Rosa de Copán are romantic relics of the past. Colonial architecture has survived in the city and in some of the villages in the mountains around it. High-quality cigars are made here primarily by hand, for export. Santa Rosa de Copán is also famous as the starting point for tours of the famous Mayan city of Copán, located just a few miles from town. Perhaps the greatest attraction for visitors is Holy Week, the weeklong events leading up to Easter. During this time of year, elaborate processions bring a solemn but festive atmosphere to the town. The charm of Holy Week is enhanced by the Old World setting of beautiful eighteenth- and nineteenth-century Spanish architecture.

8

Honduras Looks Ahead

At the beginning of the twenty-first century, Honduras faces an uncertain future. The potential for economic growth and social progress is great, but the country's past and its current environmental and social problems could drag it down again. The current government is under great political pressure. It must make good on its campaign promises to grow the economy, raise the standard of living, and quell the country's crime rate.

Predicting the future is always a risky business, especially when the subject is a country of nearly 8 million people. Predicting what will happen in faraway places and betting on the outcome, though, is what international investors do every day. Currently, these investors offer the best immediate hope for economic growth. The Honduran people themselves, however, must build on their recent successes to ensure a bright future. Before we outline the challenges to this bright future, though, let's look at reasons to be optimistic about Honduras.

Honduran democracy no longer seems to be an endangered species. Since 1982, relatively free and open elections have been held on schedule, the new constitution is well respected, and civilian-led government has been the norm. The military has been made to answer for its actions during the 1970s and 1980s. At least some of its worst crimes have been publicized and the guilty officers prosecuted. Corruption is still a problem, but recent administrations have established safeguards and watchdog groups to report and investigate allegations of paybacks or bribes, especially concerning the judicial branch of government. The role of the press as a protector of civil liberties is now understood by most citizens who have come to expect a fair degree of objectivity from the media. Hondurans now routinely criticize politicians and policies without much fear that extralegal reprisals will result. In the 2005 elections, citizens voted directly for individual members of Congress for the first time. This openness enhances the belief in a representative government. All in all, political life has improved greatly over the last several decades. This new political stability makes progress possible in social and economic spheres.

After years of struggling to rebuild in the aftermath of Hurricane Mitch, the country seems to have finally recovered. In 2007, the estimated economic growth rate was greater than 5 percent. World market prices for the country's two traditional agricultural exports, coffee and bananas, continue to fluctuate, as they always have. Recent diversification in Honduras's food exports has balanced out the effects of these market uncertainties to some extent, however. Pineapples and melons are shipped north to the United States and Canada each year in increasing numbers.

Honduran seafood is also enjoying increased market share in the United States. Like aquaculturists elsewhere, Honduran shrimp producers are now able to control the supply and quality of their product. Aquaculture is not as vulnerable to threats faced by the traditional fishing industry. Storms, coastal

Due to the increasing demand for seafood, Hondurans such as these shrimp fishermen will turn to aquaculture as a safer method for harvesting their product. By cultivating fish on man-made farms, Hondurans avoid having to deal with threats that affect the traditional fishing industry, such as water pollution and coastal development.

development, water pollution, and rise in fuel prices will not have much effect on this new class of producers. With a steady rise in global demand for seafood, it is likely that Honduras will see an expansion of its aquaculture industry.

Very good news came in 2005 when officials announced that Honduras is eligible for $1 billion in debt relief under the International Monetary Fund/World Bank's Highly Indebted Poor Countries Initiative. Reducing foreign debt payments will free government revenues and make the country more attractive to investors. The maquila, or factory production, sector of the economy continues to grow steadily. It now employs nearly one-third of the country's total industrial workers. In 2004, the assembly plants accounted for 7 percent of the gross domestic product. Ralph Lauren, Nautica, and Jockey were recently added to the long list of U.S. brands made in Honduras. Although most of the maquilas are garment plants, some much-needed diversification is taking place. Proctor and Gamble and the Lever Corporation have opened soap and cosmetics factories in Honduras, and plans are under way to bring electronics assembly plants, which will require a semiskilled workforce.

Other good news came in 2005 when Honduran leaders signed a Millennium Challenge Account compact with the United States and became the first country in the Western Hemisphere to do so. With this agreement, the United States pledged to invest $215 million to improve roads in Honduras, with the goal of diversifying and stabilizing agricultural productivity.

In 2006, U.S. Homeland Security officials announced that Puerto Cortés, the largest port in Honduras, would become the first Central American port to be included in the U.S. Container Security Initiative (CSI). The CSI is a program for enhancing and streamlining the inspection process for container vessels and their cargo headed for U.S. ports. Inclusion in CSI will speed up the time it takes to move Honduran exports to the United States and give the country an edge over its Central American competitors. With this secure transportation link in place, more U.S. investment in the country is likely.

Also in 2006, CAFTA-DR came into full force in Honduras. As the phased-in aspects of the agreement are completed in the years to come, Honduran producers will enjoy full access to one of the richest trade areas in the world. In the year before CAFTA-DR took effect, Honduran exports to the United States totaled more than $3.76 billion. By 2010, that figure had increased to 3.9 billion. At the same time, as Honduras sells more to its trading partners, U.S.- and Central America-based companies will find new opportunities to expand. The United States sold $3.64 billion in agricultural machinery, telecommunications equipment, and other industrial goods to Honduras in 2009. As tariffs and quotas are eliminated, more U.S. businesses will enter the market, especially manufacturers of consumer goods and processed foods.

CAFTA-DR certainly holds out great promise, but advocates of free trade admit they cannot know what lies ahead. Many Hondurans are concerned about domestic corn, pork, beef, poultry, and rice producers. How will they stand up under competition from U.S. producers who are some of the most efficient commercial agriculturalists in the world? Will free trade lead to even higher unemployment as small farmers go out of business? Will the maquilas lead to further, deeper investments on the part of U.S. companies? Semiskilled jobs are welcomed now, but will economic integration with North America bring anything better in the future? Many of the country's leading politicians are betting their careers on the success of CAFTA-DR.

Although most leaders believe free trade is a long-term solution to the problem of economic growth, other problems have few solutions in sight. The government struggles to solve the problem of rampant urban crime. Maras, gangs made up primarily of teenagers and young adults, have made life dangerous for residents in the bigger cities. Recently, the government implemented a get-tough policy against their criminal activity. Its success was limited, however, by human rights organizations charging that the crackdown was a threat to constitutional civil liberties enjoyed by Hondurans.

Other, much older, problems persist, as well. Despite the recent economic growth, almost one-third of Honduran children under the age of five are malnourished. Nearly 40 percent of the population lives on less than $3 a day, and about half the people live below the poverty line. The unemployment rate is estimated to be a low 3 percent, yet about 60 percent of the population continues to live below the poverty line. Most people hold jobs, but wages remain very low. Clean drinking water, adequate health care, and education are all pressing concerns for many Hondurans. Working with various international aid groups, such as the United States Agency for International Development (USAID), Honduras has programs in place to address the old problems of underdevelopment and the new problem of competitiveness introduced with CAFTA-DR.

INTERNATIONAL DEVELOPMENT ASSISTANCE

The USAID has much experience in Honduras. In the past, it has administered basic assistance projects such as the Food for Peace program, which helped alleviate the problem of malnutrition in Honduras's rural areas. The goal of the agency's current regional strategy is to help Honduras maximize trade opportunities under CAFTA-DR. In addition to programs aimed at economic growth, others fund environmental, health, and education initiatives that are necessary if Honduras's current growth is to continue.

In environmental management and disaster planning, USAID funds the creation of geographic information systems (GIS) for natural resource management. With the terrible lessons of Mitch in mind, U.S. consultants train local officials in disaster preparedness. For example, they teach Honduran officials to monitor river flow data in order to provide early warning in case of rapid river rise. Community leaders also receive training in evacuation and emergency food and shelter planning.

Other programs are aimed at improving the basic health and education of people in rural areas. Disease control and monitoring, especially of HIV/AIDS, is a priority even though the HIV infection rate in Honduras was a low 0.8 percent in 2008. During recent years, the country began to see progress in controlling malaria, Chagas disease, and other debilitating diseases. In a 2005 list of the top 40 countries in the world with the highest infection rates of AIDS, Honduras was the only Central American country listed. Family planning and AIDS awareness programs were part of the successful effort to bring this problem under control.

In education, young people from low-income families are the focus of new alternative delivery systems for preschool, primary, and secondary students. Teacher training is already

Education is a major issue in Honduras, where under 50 percent of children are enrolled in public schools. Here, Honduran children attend class in a makeshift school outside the capital of Tegucigalpa.

improving the quality of public education in some urban schools. At the national level, consultants work with the government to develop countrywide standards, testing, and evaluation methods.

Another U.S. agency, the U.S. Peace Corps, has been active in Honduras for many years. About 230 volunteers, one of the largest contingents stationed anywhere in the world, currently work in small towns and villages on public health, sanitation, education, and construction projects.

WORKING FROM THE GROUND UP

An example of the work being done to assist in the transition to an open market system is the USAID project that focuses on small farmers. With the coming of CAFTA, small growers need to become more competitive to survive. Many fear that once U.S. food products are widely available in Honduras, these growers will be thrown out of work, thereby swelling the ranks of unemployment. Traditional farmers have expertise in growing crops for local markets. They do not, however, have the networks or experience in producing export-quality crops.

A pilot program was established to provide assistance for these small growers in marketing, postharvest handling, processing, and the use of new technology. Since sweet potatoes are grown by many farmers, that crop was chosen for the pilot. Development workers saw an opportunity for small growers to build an export strategy for this product. Trade specialists working with USAID identified potential buyers in the Netherlands and Canada, and a group of farmers in northern Honduras were invited to participate. They were introduced to several new technologies such as drip irrigation. This allowed them to bring more land under cultivation, and contracts with an exporter were signed. By the end of the first year, 45 farmers had joined the program, and 520,000 pounds (235,868 kilograms) of sweet potatoes had been shipped to Europe. Each of the growers made an average of $3,375 per acre ($1,350 per hectare) in profits, an increase of about 50 percent over the previous year. Almost 150 new jobs were created, and these small farmers are now participating in the global agricultural market. Although this is a modest success, the hope is that programs like this will give farmers and others the confidence to compete.

Apart from further industrial and agricultural development inspired by CAFTA-DR, what business possibilities lie ahead for Honduras? Tourism appears to offer the greatest potential for growth. The tourist industry is the single-largest sector of the global economy. It already contributes to the local economy of some areas in Honduras, such as the North Coast and the Bay Islands. So many more tourists might come if certain key issues could be resolved. The chronically high unemployment rate and the accompanying crime problem must be settled. Convincing tourists that travel is safe is a necessary step.

With careful planning and a little luck with its CAFTA-DR growth, Honduras could become the next Costa Rica, a world-class ecotourist destination. It has the same forested mountains, mysterious lagoons, beaches, and exotic wildlife that have contributed to Costa Rica's success. Developing ecotourism would bring in foreign currency and encourage the preservation of threatened natural areas and wildlife. As tourism grows, Honduras's cultural attractions also would draw visitors not interested in mountain trails or scuba diving.

More than other countries in Central America, Honduras faces an uncertain future. Many problems remain to be solved. The country could backslide and return to the bad old days of dictators, hopelessness, and poverty. So much has been accomplished in such a relatively short time, though. Thirty years ago, no one could have predicted that Honduras would be where it is today. After centuries in which its history and even its geography seemed to work against it, Honduras is now poised to make the most of its past.

Physical Geography

Location Central America, between Guatemala and Nicaragua, bordering the Caribbean Sea and the Gulf of Honduras on the north and to the south bordering the Gulf of Fonseca between El Salvador and Nicaragua

Area 43,277 square miles (112,087 square kilometers), slightly larger than the state of Tennessee; *land:* 43,201 square miles (111,890 square kilometers); *water:* 77 square miles (200 square kilometers)

Boundaries 945 miles (1,520 kilometers) of land border; Guatemala, 159 miles (256 kilometers), El Salvador, 213 miles (342 kilometers), Nicaragua, 573 miles (922 kilometers); coastline: 510 miles (820 kilometers)

Climate Tropical wet in Caribbean lowlands, temperate in the highlands, tropical wet and dry in Pacific lowlands

Terrain Mostly mountains in interior, narrow coastal plains

Elevation Extremes Lowest point is the Caribbean Sea, sea level; highest point is Cerro Las Minas 9,416 feet (2,870 meters)

Land Use arable land, 9.53%; permanent crops, 3.21%; other, 87.26% (2005)

Irrigated Land 309 square miles (800 square kilometers) (2003)

Natural Hazards Frequent, but generally mild, earthquakes; extremely susceptible to damaging hurricanes and floods along the Caribbean coast

Natural Resources Timber, gold, silver, copper, lead, zinc, iron ore, fish, hydropower

Environmental Issues Urban population expanding; deforestation results from logging and the clearing of land for agricultural purposes; further land degradation and soil erosion hastened by uncontrolled development and improper land use practices such as farming of marginal lands; mining activities polluting Lago de Yojoa (the country's largest source of freshwater), as well as several rivers and streams, with heavy metals

People

Population 8,143,564 (2011 estimate); males, 4,095,913; females, 4,047,651

Population Density 185 per square mile (72 per square kilometer)

Population Growth Rate	1,888% (2011 est.)
Net Migration Rate	-1.25 migrant(s)/1,000 population (2011 est.)
Total Fertility Rate	3.09 children born/woman (2.1 is replacement rate) (2011 est.)
Birthrate	25.14 births/1,000 population (2011 est.)
Death Rate	5.02 deaths/1,000 population (2011 est.)
Life Expectancy at Birth	Total Population: 70.61 years (male, 68.93 years; female, 72.37 years)
Median Age	Total: 21 years (male, 20.6 years; female, 21.4 years)
Age Structure	0–14 years, 36.7%; 15–64 years, 59.5%; 65 years and over, 3.8%
Settlement	50% rural, 50% urban (2010 est.)
Racial and Ethnic Groups	Mestizo (mixed Amerindian and European) 90%, Amerindian 7%, black 2%, white 1%
Religions	Roman Catholic 97%, Protestant 3%
Languages	Spanish, Amerindian dialects
Literacy	(Age 15 and older can read and write) Total population, 80% (male, 79.8%) (female, 80.2%) (2001 census)
Human Development Index	112 (among 182 countries ranked)

Economy

Currency	Lempira (HNL); US $1=18.9 HNL (2010)
GDP Purchasing Power Parity	$36.63 billion (2010 est.)
GDP (Official Exchange Rate)	$15.35 billion (2010 est.)
GDP Per Capita	$4,200 (2010 est.)
Labor Force	3.394 million (2010 est.)
Population below Poverty Line	65% (2010)
Unemployment	5.1% (2010 est.)
Gross Domestic Product (GDP)	$8.478 billion (2006 est.)
Rate of Economic Growth	2.8% (2010 est.)
Labor Force by Occupation	Services, 39.8%; agriculture, 39.2%; industry, 20.9% (2005 est.)
GDP Composition by section	Services, 60.8%; agriculture, 12.4%; industry, $26.9% (2010 est.)
Agricultural Products	Coffee, bananas, shrimp and lobster, citrus, corn, tilapia, beef, timber

Industries	Textiles and apparel, wood products, cigars, sugar, coffee
Exports	$5.879 billion f.o.b. (2010 est.)
Export Commodities	Apparel, coffee, bananas, shrimp, palm oil, cigars, lobster, fruit, lumber, wire harnesses
Imports	$8.878 billion f.o.b. (2010 est.)
Import Commodities	Machinery and transport equipment, industrial raw materials, chemical products, fuels, food stuffs
Leading Trade Partners	*Exports:* U.S., 40.9%; El Salvador, 8.6%; Guatemala, 7.2%; *Imports:* U.S., 33.9%; Guatemala, 10.5%; Mexico, 6.8%; El Salvador, 6.2%; China, 4.7%; Costa Rica, 4.67%. (2009)

Government

Country Name	Conventional long form: Republic of Honduras; conventional short form: Honduras; local long form: Republica de Honduras; local short form: Honduras
Capital City	Tegucigalpa
Type of Government	Democratic constitutional republic
Independence	September 15, 1821 (from Spain)
Administrative Divisions	18 departments (departamentos, singular– departamento); Atlantida, Choluteca, Colon, Comayagua, Copán, Cortes, El Paraiso, Francisco Morazan, Gracias a Dios, Intibuca, Islas de la Bahia, La Paz, Lempira, Ocotepeque, Olancho, Santa Barbara, Valle, Yoro
Constitution	January 11, 1982; effective January 20, 1982; amended many times

Infrastructure

Transportation	Roadways: 8,453 miles (13,600 km.) of which 1,724 miles (2,775 km.) are paved (2000); Railways: 434 miles (699 km.); Airports: 106–12 with paved runways; Waterways: 289 miles (465 km.), most navigable only to small craft (Faces both Atlantic and Pacific oceans)
Communications	Phones: 7.04 million (825,800 main lines; 6,211,000 cell phones) (2008) Radio broadcast stations: 306 (AM 241, FM 53, short-wave 12 (1998); Television broadcast stations: 14 (2010) Internet users: 658,500 (2008) * Source: *CIA-The World Factbook* (2011)

1502	Christopher Columbus sails along eastern shore of Central America, stopping briefly at the Bay Islands and the mainland, naming the region *Honduras*.
1524–1526	Cortes conquers the Amerindian people of Honduras and establishes the town of Trujillo on the Caribbean coast.
1537	Comayagua is founded.
1545	The Audiencia of Guatemala is created. A regional arm of the Viceroyalty of New Spain, this audiencia holds jurisdiction over Honduras until its independence in the nineteenth century.
1578	Tegucigalpa is founded.
1821	Independence from Spain is declared by the Central American colonies. Negotiations begin among them about a new form of government.
1823	United Provinces of Central America (UPCA) is formed by Honduras, Guatemala, El Salvador, Costa Rica, and Nicaragua.
1838	UPCA dissolves. Honduras becomes an independent republic.
1862–1876	Civil wars and coups destabilize the country.
1876–1883	Liberal reforms expand foreign investment; land concessions to foreign banana companies begins.
1890–1920	United Fruit Company and Standard Fruit Company control most aspects of banana production in Honduras and interfere in national politics.
1919	United States directly intervenes militarily for the first time to protect banana company plantations.
1924	United States again sends troops into the country to quell revolts.
1933	General Tiburcio Carias assumes dictatorial powers and rules Honduras until 1948.
1954	National labor strike led by banana workers paralyzes Honduras. The United States and Honduras sign a military treaty allowing U.S. military exercises in country.
1955	Honduran women are given the right to vote.
1969	"Soccer War" breaks out between Honduras and El Salvador.

1975	"Bananagate" scandal is made public. (Finance minister accepted $1.2 million bribe from United Brands.)
1982–1984	U.S. military aid to Honduras increases as the country becomes involved in the Nicaraguan Contra War.
1986	Anti-U.S. protests over Contra War and atrocities committed by CIA-backed Honduran forces pressure the new Honduran government to distance itself from the United States. Protests continue sporadically for next two years.
1990	President Callejas implements International Monetary Fund's free market program in the face of popular opposition.
1998	Carlos Roberto Flores Facussé takes office as president and takes measures to modernize the economy and raise the standard of living, still one of the lowest in the Western Hemisphere. Hurricane Mitch brings devastation to Central America, killing thousands of people in the region, creating millions of homeless, and destroying most of Honduras's roads, bridges, and rail lines.
2004	Honduras signs the Central American Free Trade Agreement (CAFTA) with the United States, Guatemala, El Salvador, Costa Rica, and Nicaragua. The Dominican Republic is included in the pact the following year.
2006	CAFTA enters into force in Honduras.
2007	Longstanding territorial dispute between Honduras and Nicaragua settled by the International Court of Justice.
2008	Honduras joins an alliance of leftist leaders in Latin America headed by Venezuelan President Hugo Chavez, thereby breaking long-standing close ties with the United States.
2009	President Zelaya is removed from office by the military and forced into exile following which Roberto Micheletti is appointed acting president and U.S. suspends all aid to country. In November, Porfirio "Pepe" Lobo Sosa, candidate of the Conservative National Party, wins presidential election.
2010	Porfirio Lobo sworn in as president and deposed president, Manuel Zelaya, goes into exile in the Dominican Republic.

125

Bibliography

Books

Peter N. Stearns, ed. *Encyclopedia of World History* (sixth edition). Boston: Houghton Mifflin Company, 2001.

Global Economic Prospects and the Developing Countries. Washington, D.C.: The World Bank, 2002.

Merriam-Webster's Geographical Dictionary (third edition) Springfield, Mass.: Merriam-Webster, Incorporated, 1998.

Web sites

CIA World Factbook, Honduras
http://www.cia.gov/cia/publications/factbook/geos/gt.html

Country Reports
http://www.countryreports.org/

World Bank, Honduras Data Profile
http://devdata.worldbank.org

Countries and Their Cultures
http://www.everyculture.com/index.html

About.com
http://geography.about.com/sitesearch.htm

U.S. Department of State, Background Note: Honduras
http://www.state.gov/r/pa/ei/bgn/1922.htm

U.S. Department of State, Consular General Information Sheet, Honduras
http://travel.state.gov/honduras.html

Books

Andrews, Edward Wyllys, and William Leonard Fash, eds. *Copán: The History of an Ancient Mayan Kingdom.* Santa Fe, N.M.: School of American Research, 2005.

Chandler, Gary, and Liza Prado Chandler. *Honduras and the Bay Islands.* Victoria, Australia: Lonely Planet, 2007.

Crosby, Alfred W. *The Columbian Exchange: Biological and Cultural Consequences of 1492.* Westport, Conn.: Greenwood Press, 1972.

Liu, Kam-biu, and Richard J. Murname. *Hurricanes and Typhoons: Past, Present, and Future.* New York: Columbia University Press, 2004.

Panet, Jean-Pierre. *Honduras Guide.* Cold Spring Harbor, N.Y.: Open Road, 2002.

Striffler, Steve, and Mark Moberg. *Banana Wars.* Durham, N.C.: Duke University Press, 2003.

Williams, Robert G. *States and Social Evolution: Coffee and the Rise of National Governments in Central America.* Chapel Hill: University of North Carolina Press, 1994.

Web sites

Embassy of Honduras
http://www.hondurasemb.org/

Hurricane Mitch Reports
http://www.hurricanemitch.com/

National Geographic: Honduras
http://www3.nationalgeographic.com/places/countries/country_honduras.html

Organization of American States (OAS)
http://www.oas.org/

U.S. Agency for International Development
http://www.usaid.gov/locations/latin_america_caribbean/

Photo Credits

page:

10: © Lucidity Information Design, LLC
13: Daniel Leclair/Reuters/Landov
17: © Lucidity Information Design, LLC
22: © Tim Wright/CORBIS
26: © Yann Arthus-Bertrand/CORBIS
36: AP images
42: © CORBIS
45: Scala/Art Resource, NY
53: Time Life Pictures/Getty Images
61: Sandra A. Dunlap/www.shutterstock.com
67: AFP/Getty Images

75: AFP/Getty Images
80: Greg E. Mathieson/ MAI/Landov
85: AFP/Getty Images
89: AFP/Getty Images
94: Reuters/Landov
100: Tomas Bravo/Reuters/Landov
102: AP Images
105: AFP/Getty Images
110: AFP/Getty Images
114: © Lynda Richardson/CORBIS
118: Tomas Bravo/Reuters/Landov

Index

ROGER E. DENDINGER was born in New Orleans, Louisiana, and grew up there and in Mobile, Alabama. He is associate professor of geography at the South Dakota School of Mines and Technology in Rapid City, South Dakota. In addition to teaching and writing, he enjoys hiking and biking in the Black Hills, where he lives with his wife, Amy; their three sons, Zac, Nash, and Gabe; and their daughter, Julia Bereket.

CHARLES F. GRITZNER is Distinguished Professor Emeritus of Geography at South Dakota State University in Brookings. In 2010, he retired after a 50-year career of college teaching. He enjoys travel, writing, and sharing his love for and knowledge of geography with readers. Gritzner has contributed to Chelsea House's MODERN WORLD NATIONS, MAJOR WORLD CULTURES, EXTREME ENVIRONMENTS, and GLOBAL CONNECTIONS series. He has served as both President and Executive Director of the National Council for Geographic Education (NCGE) and has received the Council's highest honor, the George J. Miller Award for Distinguished Service to Geographic Education, as well as numerous other national teaching, service, and research recognitions from the NCGE, the Association of American Geographers, and other organizations. Gritzner lives in South Dakota with his wife, Yvonne, and their "family" of two Italian Greyhounds.